THE
LOGOS
STORY

THE LOGOS
STORY

ELAINE RHOTON

*Photo acknowledgements: Susanna Burton, Peter Conlan,
Warwick Cooper, Canon K.W: Coates, Scottish Daity Express
and Martin Keiller.*

British Library Cataloguing in Publication Data

Rhoton. Elaine
    The Logos Story
    1. Christian overseas mission
    I. Title
    266.023

    ISBN 0-9630908-4-4

Published by OM LIT
             P.O. Box 1047
             Waynesboro, GA 30830

Printed in Colombia

IMPRESO EN COLOMBIA
BUENA SEMILLA
Apartado 29724
Bogota, Colombia

CONTENTS

Dedicated to
Bjørn Kristiansen (1934–1987),
John Yarr (1924–1980)
and
George Paget (1911–1978)
whose faith and commitment God used in
shaping the Logos *ministry.*

Prologue

Judith Fredricsen, a vivacious, attractive young woman from New Zealand, moved restlessly in the narrow hospital bed. The constant creaking and groaning sounds that accompany a ship making its way through rough waters lent an eerie quality to the atmosphere. And the events of the previous day kept crowding into her mind. An adventure-filled outing to the mountains of Argentina had ended in disaster as she had tripped and fallen, bruising herself badly against the sharp rocks. Unable to walk properly, she was helped back to the *Logos* by her companions. There the ship's doctor cleaned her up, bound her injured leg and ordered her to bed.

On the following morning the leg had looked bad. The doctor had taken her to the hospital for X-rays. A torn ligament was diagnosed and the swollen, discoloured leg was immobilised in a half-cast.

Now Judith lay alone in the unfamiliar surroundings of the ship's hospital where she had been put so that she could rest undisturbed. Rest? If only she *could* drop off to sleep! Suddenly she recoiled in shock as a long loud crunching noise pierced the room—the sound of metal grinding against rock. A feeling of nausea engulfed Judith as she sensed this was something serious. 'What a stupid

time to have my leg in a cast!' she thought impatiently.
Sitting up and lifting her legs over the side of the bed, she
prepared to get up and try to find out what had happened.

After fifteen months aboard the *Logos*, Bagus Surjantoro
from Indonesia felt very much at home on the ship. The
people who worked on the ship had become his 'family'
and he felt very close to them. This particular evening he
had spent in his office, the programme room, trying to
finalise the planning for conferences in the next port.
About 10.30 p.m. Nimrod Twanie, a cheerful, unassuming black South African, popped into the office and pulled
him away from his work to go and practise with their
newly-formed quartet. In the studio Nimrod was insistent
that they practise a song that had been running through
his mind all day—the old familiar English hymn, 'Rock of
Ages'.

'Look, man,' exclaimed Bagus impatiently, 'there's a
conference on evangelism coming up on Thursday and we
need to have something to sing at it. "Rock of Ages"
doesn't have anything to do with the theme.'

In the end they decided to compromise. First they sang
'Rock of Ages' and then went on to practise something
else for the next hour or so. It was a small incident that
was to have special meaning for them later on.

By that time it was getting quite late—time to get to
bed, they decided. Bagus stopped by the office to make
sure everything was in order before going on to the cabin
which he shared with eleven other young men. He
undressed quietly and climbed into his bunk, read a passage from his Bible and prayed. By the time he finally
crawled under the blankets to go to sleep, it was nearly
midnight. Suddenly there was a loud crash and the ship
came to a grinding halt. An instant of stunned silence
followed. Then the men began jumping out of bed, looking at one another uncertainly and asking excitedly, '*Que
pasó? Que pasó?* What's happened?'

Before every voyage Linda Wells became irritable and depressed, as she tried to cope with waves of fear that threatened to paralyse her. She recalled in vivid detail the events of the previous voyage when the *Logos* had run into bad weather and was caught broadside by a huge wave. The sudden tipping of the ship sent furniture sliding across the floor of Linda's cabin. Drawers fell out, and books were flung from the shelves. Linda had screamed in panic.

The next day she felt angry at her fears, angry at the ship and perhaps even a bit angry at God. Going up on deck, she cried to him, 'Lord, I just can't trust my life to this tub of metal!'

A calm, still voice in her mind seemed to answer, 'You're not trusting your life to this tub of metal. You're trusting it to me.'

Her fears receded and peace returned.

Some time later she learned that the ship was not going to travel through the Magellan Straits as she had thought, but was going farther south around the tip of South America. All the old feelings of fear and insecurity flooded back. Oppressed by a grim sense of foreboding, she talked to the captain and to her husband, Graham, begging them to take the ship another route. Both tried to reassure her. Still looking for a way out, she went to the ship's doctor.

'Look,' she said, 'we'll be four days at sea and I always get dreadfully seasick. I'm pregnant now and that can't be good for the baby. Shouldn't I go overland to the next port?'

'No, Linda,' replied the doctor. 'You've already had one miscarriage. I think it would be best for you to be on board where I can look after you.'

After much inner conflict, Linda decided finally that she had to accept the doctor's judgement.

The ship set sail from Ushuaia, Argentina in the evening. Surprisingly enough Linda felt relatively peaceful.

Nevertheless, she felt she should pack a small bag of warm clothes, cookies, and juice for her small daughter Aimee; almost, she thought later, as though she had known what was about to happen. That done, she crawled into bed fully dressed, much to the amusement of her husband. As she lay in bed she murmured, 'Lord, I don't really feel afraid. Why am I doing all this?'

Again she heard that still, small voice saying, 'Linda, I'm going to do something that will totally amaze you.'

Drifting off to sleep, Linda thought absently, 'Well, that either means we're going to be shipwrecked or we're going to get a better ship.'

Two hours later Linda was jolted to consciousness by the loud, harsh sound of the ship scraping against rock. She leapt up out of bed instantly, springing over her husband Graham. Grabbing the bag she had packed and a warm coat, she reached up to pull Aimee from the top bunk.

'Now don't overreact,' cautioned Graham, as he stood dazed and dopey from sleep, unable to believe what had happened. 'We've probably just let off the pilot.'

Suppressing a little spurt of irritation at what she considered an inane remark, Linda opened the cabin door and walked out, pausing only to say to Graham, 'When you're ready, would you mind bringing up the life-jackets?'

It was just before midnight on 4 January, 1988. For the *Logos* it was the beginning of the end.

1
Beginnings

In the late 1950s nothing could have been farther from the minds of George Verwer and those with him than the idea of a ship. They were just a small group of Bible college students in the Chicago area. Their dominant thought at that moment was how to get some sort of vehicle to transport them and their stuff down to Mexico for the holidays. For penniless students that was a problem of major proportions. Yet they were set on spending their summer vacation in Mexico; but not to stretch out lazily on white sandy beaches in the bright sunshine after a refreshing swim in inviting blue waters. They had something more important in mind.

Mexico, they had been told, was a land full of religious people who believed firmly in God. Yet few of them realised that it was possible to know God in a personal way. They were missing out on the most important experience in life! That was a tragic situation which should be remedied, thought the students. 'We can't do the whole job,' they told themselves, 'but we'll do our part.'

Great ideals, but how could they be put into practice without the use of a couple of cars or a small van? The students didn't see any solution, but they reasoned that the work was God's work, so he was the one who should provide the answer. Many hours were spent in prayer, asking him to do so.

A young man who came to their weekly prayer times heard them praying for a vehicle. Immediately his thoughts went to his uncle who had a fleet of trucks. Perhaps he would have one he could let the students use for the trip.

'Oh yes,' the uncle replied when the young man asked him about it. 'See that old truck over there on the blocks. They can have that one if they want it, but I can tell you, it will never make it out of Chicago, much less down to Mexico.'

A few days later the truck, packed with students, Christian books and tracts, was headed toward Mexico. Not only did it make the trip safely to Mexico and back, it made the trip twice more in subsequent summers.

In the early sixties the same scene on a larger scale was taking place in Europe. The students had graduated. Two or three had moved down to Mexico to work there. Others had turned their attention to Europe. The goal was the same: to get people excited about knowing God in a personal way. The method was the same as well: distributing Christian literature and getting into conversation with individuals. Trying to find transport was a recurring problem too.

The most daunting thought to the young people was that Europe was so big and varied! What impact could a couple of dozen men and women have? Clearly their contribution was vital, but it just was not enough. How could they get more—many more—people involved?

'By getting the already existing churches involved! That's the answer,' thought George Verwer. 'When we go into a city, instead of attempting to do all the work ourselves, we'll try to get people from various churches to work with us. Once these people become personally involved and see how God can use them, they will want to continue on even after we've left to go somewhere else.'

That was the beginning of the organisation known as Operation Mobilisation, which soon became better known as OM. The idea of mobilising God's people to reach needy, lost and hurting people in Europe began to catch fire. Each summer several hundred young people from a wide range of churches would meet together for a few days of orientation and training and then divide up into small teams. Laden with sleeping bags, air mattresses and lots of Christian literature, they would fan out to different parts of Europe and work with interested churches in those areas. Sometimes the teams would pitch tents in camping areas. Often they would simply put down their sleeping bags on the floors of the church building and camp out there.

Even though the lifestyle was very simple, money was still a major problem. Most of the young people had none themselves and OM had no money to pay them or even to provide for their expenses. Their churches and interested Christian friends provided the necessary funds. When this was not enough, and often it wasn't, the young people prayed that God would provide from other sources. He always did provide what was really necessary, but never enough to indulge in luxurious living.

In the autumn of 1963 the first OM team set out for India. Instead of working for a few weeks in the summer, this group of young people—by this time known as OMers—planned to remain for one or two years. Each autumn a new group would head out from Europe to replace the people who were returning.

Just as with the original team going to Mexico, transport was a problem. Flying the young people to India was never even considered. There was no money for that kind of transport. Instead, the OMers went overland in ancient, battered, loaded-to-the-brim trucks. It was a gruelling two-month trip through mountains deep with snow and across bleak, barren wastelands, sometimes on tracks that could hardly be distinguished as roads.

Jolting up and down in the back of one of these trucks, George Verwer squirmed to try to find a less uncomfortable position. Impatient to reach India and fretting at all the time being wasted in doing nothing but travelling, George began to reflect on the situation. 'There must be a better way,' he thought. Some way to cut down on expenses, which in George's eyes were exorbitant in spite of the simple, somewhat primitive style of travel. 'What would be ideal,' he thought, 'would be some way to combine travelling with the ministry of distributing Christian literature and talking with people about Jesus Christ.' As he considered the matter, an idea began to germinate in his mind.

A few months later he was relaxing with several OM leaders back in England. As the conversation drifted from topic to topic, someone mentioned the idea of using a ship for evangelism.

'That's what we need!' exclaimed George, seizing the idea with great excitement. 'Just imagine what we could do with a ship! I've been thinking of this for some months now and man, the possibilities stagger my mind! Think of the money that could be saved in travel alone!'

He began to elaborate about how money would be saved and how travel-time by ship could be put to good use instead of being wasted as it was by overland travel. His enthusiasm was contagious. Soon everyone in the room was throwing out ideas—some wild, some witty, but many quite serious. Afterwards some wondered if it was here that the name *Logos* ('Word') was first suggested, but no one could remember for certain.

Encouraged by this response, George decided to present the idea to a larger group of OM leaders. These people knew George to be a man brimming with creativity; he could spout out original ideas, colourful phrases, and humorous remarks as easily as other people turn the pages of a book. Often his ideas showed unusual perception and vision; the development of OM bore testimony to this repeatedly. Other times they were wild to the point of utter impracticability or even absurdity. But they were interesting—always very interesting.

So when George began to present his idea of an ocean-going ship, there was an almost tangible feeling of anticipation among the listeners. Even George's most serious statements were often interspersed with humorous side-remarks guaranteed to send an audience into convulsions of laughter. And laugh they did this time. But along with the laughter was a serious attempt to evaluate George's idea. This time it was relegated to the realm of far-out ideas; too impractical, too unrealistic ever to work.

George, however, was reluctant to let go of the idea. Hearing about an old ship up for sale in Sweden, he decided to go and see it. As he explored its interior, his mind boggled at the thought of all that could be done with facilities such as these. At that time no one wanted old ships; there was too much work involved in keeping them seaworthy. So they were selling at very low prices. This particular ship, which could carry about one hundred people, was selling at £25,000. 'How can this be?' thought George in wonder. His mind went back to the hundreds of old battered trucks which OM had bought cheaply and put into workable condition for transporting OMers over the years.

George became completely convinced that OM should get a ship. Not the one he had just seen, but some ship that would be suitable for the use he had in mind. More thought would have to be given about the kind of ship that was needed. The first step, however, was to convince other people of the incredible potential he saw. To clarify his ideas and make them widely known, he began to put them down on paper.

A year passed. Nothing happened. Two years passed. Still nothing happened. Hardly a person in the shipping world showed any interest at all. Of the response he did get, at least eighty per cent was negative. From one of the main OM leaders in India he got a strongly worded letter condemning this 'wildcat scheme' and saying in effect: 'Here we are in India battling to get gospel tracts. What are you doing in London thinking about blowing a load of money on a hunk of scrap?'

Why have an ocean-going ship for world evangelism? read the caption on the leaflet. Intrigued, a young man in naval uniform picked up the paper and began to read. In those moments an interest was aroused that was to significantly affect the realisation of the ship's project.

The young man was an up-and-coming officer in the merchant navy of Great Britain. The seafaring life offers enormous temptations in the form of loose women, alcohol, and many other things, yet this man had a clear testimony as a Christian. Serving as first officer with a large company, he was already qualified as a captain and had every prospect of advancement. But after a long correspondence with George Verwer and much prayer, he left his lucrative career to work with OM for a month. He wasn't sure OM was the right place for him, but he was willing to investigate. In 1966 he committed himself to the ship's project.

God had provided exactly the right team to turn the vision of a ship into reality. The British captain was able to provide the professional expertise necessary and his very presence gave the venture a sense of solidity, sanity and credibility. On the other hand, George Verwer had the vision and the dynamism to keep the project moving forward.

Blond, handsome, immaculately dressed in a dark suit and bow tie, standing stiffly erect, the young naval officer was the personification of a proper British sea captain. From his perspective, there was only one way to do a thing in the shipping world and that was the 'proper' way. With his training and experience he knew just what should be done and how to do it.

A more complete contrast than George Verwer was hardly imaginable. Thin, wiry, perpetually in motion, whether mentally or physically, George was a veritable dynamo. To him, excellence was great but the top priority was action. Added to this was the fact that, as he launched the idea of a ship, he was almost totally ignorant of marine matters. However, he soon developed a voracious appetite for all kinds of information about shipping, reading everything he could lay hands on, visiting ships, talking with people in the shipping world. He even sailed with an Indian Christian pilot bringing ships into Bombay, India, and got the officer to explain all sorts of things about ships.

This vast difference in personality and perspective inevitably led to equally vast differences in opinion. Being the only professional seaman among the OMers, the British captain often felt like 'a man among boys', as he put it. How could he communicate with colleagues who didn't have the background to understand and appreciate the significance of what he had to say? Questions constantly arose about the vessel. What sort of features in a ship were necessary in order to fulfil the ministry that was evolving in the minds of George and the other OMers? Which of these were actually feasible? Which were the impractical dreams of people ignorant of shipping matters? More difficult yet were questions about the crew. Should these be only professionals? Should they be paid a salary? And the most sensitive question of all: who would be in authority? Who would have the final say? The captain, or George Verwer as director of OM?

These were questions that could not be answered easily. The OM ship would be unique, vastly different from the normal ship in the world of commerce. No one could visualise exactly how the ship would function because such a thing had never been attempted before, at least, not on the scale that George and the captain had in mind.

In the four years following the captain's commitment to the project he and George spoke separately or together in hundreds of meetings. Each time they would share in glowing words their vision for a ship and would challenge Christians to pray for it. People began to get excited and to accept the challenge to pray.

Of course, there were practical matters to consider as well. A suitable vessel at an acceptable price had to be found. Even more difficult than that, professional seamen must be found—men who were willing to leave highly-paid jobs for a ship ministry that didn't even exist as yet.

In the wisdom of God and by his power the ship was to come into being and have a ministry that would alter the course of thousands of lives around the world. However, it did not develop in the way George Verwer and the others had expected. George had first thought of a ship as a way to transport workers to India, but the ship was never used significantly for this purpose. The British captain had given credibility to the project and had seemed to personify it, inspiring many professional seamen to commit themselves to the ship, yet he never actually sailed as her captain.

2
Now is the hour

Young, robust, full of vitality, and eager to sample all life
had to offer, Bjørn Kristiansen flew out to take command
of a Norwegian oil tanker operating in Indonesia. Four
years later he was back in Norway—this time in a hospital
bed. His strange illness with its bewildering, disturbing
weakness, was diagnosed as a serious case of oedema,
which meant that fluids were collecting in his legs because
of a heart defect. A couple of operations, instead of
bringing the hoped-for improvement, left him in a coma
for weeks. Periodically, tests were made to make sure his
brain was still functioning. He was not expected to live.

During one of these tests weeks after the last operation,
Bjørn unexpectedly returned to consciousness. A big tube
thrust down his throat prevented him from making any
sound, but the nurse had noticed a change in him and
began to talk softly and calmly to him. He was very ill, she
told him. Quite possibly he could die. But if he would put
his trust in the Lord Jesus, he would receive eternal life
and would live forever with him.

Bjørn was not really interested in this kind of talk. Like
most young men he had lived without a serious thought
about God. Not that he was anti-God. God just didn't
seem important to him. Even now, facing death, Bjørn

had no interest in hearing about God and wished the nurse would stop talking. At the same time he sensed the nurse was genuinely concerned about him and he appreciated that concern. When she finally said, 'I'll pray for you', he gave an almost imperceptible nod of politeness, thinking she had at last finished.

But she hadn't. Her words were not just a polite way of ending the conversation. Standing by the bed, she began to pray. Suddenly Bjørn was gripped with the awareness that God was real to this woman; she was talking to someone she knew well; and she was pleading for him— Bjørn. A yearning welled up inside him to know God as she did, to sense God's reality and closeness as she did. From deep in his heart he cried out with longing to God. And as the nurse finished praying, Bjørn knew that God was there in the room with them.

That afternoon the tubes were removed from Bjørn's body and he was able to swallow a bit of food and water. For the first time in many months he could turn his body, plagued with bed sores, and sleep on his side. What a feeling of relief! The next day he could sit on the edge of the bed and dangle his feet. Soon he started the process of learning to walk again. He was transferred from the intensive care unit to an ordinary hospital ward.

Certainly Bjørn had every reason to be in high spirits, but he wasn't. On the contrary, he was deeply depressed. He knew Jesus had touched his life, but this very fact seemed to contribute to his depression. Vivid pictures of his past life kept forcing themselves into his mind, each one adding to a growing awareness of the sinful life he had led. He felt crushed by an oppressive weight of guilt.

Finally, in desperation he said to himself, 'I've got to find someone I can talk to!' Slipping stealthily out of the hospital that evening, he found a taxi and directed it to a seamen's mission in the city. There he introduced himself and announced that he had just run away from the hospital. The pastor invited him into the house and phoned the hospital to regulate matters. Then he settled into a chair and invited Bjørn to unburden himself. The flood-gate was lifted and a frothing, turbulent torrent of words and emotion gushed out as Bjørn began to talk about his past life.

'Just a minute,' the pastor interrupted after listening attentively. 'It's about time you got to know what God says about people in your situation.' Opening his Bible, he read passage after passage explaining the terrible sin and guilt of men and what Jesus had done about it. For the first time in his life, Bjørn heard the 'Good News' of the Bible, that Jesus had died to pay the penalty for sin, so that people could have forgiveness. He finally understood that Jesus was alive today and that it was possible to follow him and entrust one's life into his hands. The pastor put the crucial question to him bluntly, 'Now that you know Jesus has touched your life and is calling you to follow him, what are you going to do about it?'

Bjørn decided to accept the challenge and follow Jesus. He and the pastor prayed together. When Bjørn left the mission hall, he was a new person. In fact, he was so new that everyone noticed it. Even the hospital records noted the change from a prolonged state of depression to ela-tion.

One week later, on 26 October, 1967, Bjørn was dis-charged from the hospital. He went home determined to make a break with his old lifestyle. Friends viewed him sceptically and predicted it would last no more than a few days—a month, at most. They were wrong. Instead, God was to use Bjørn Kristiansen in a significant way to help launch the ministry of the MV *Logos*.

After a few months Bjørn had recovered and returned to sea in Indonesia. There he met many Christians and became involved extensively in various Christian activities. As he did, he began to visualise a small ship that would be used to carry the good news of Jesus Christ to the 13,000 islands of Indonesia. In 1970 he returned to

Norway to try to get such a ship. During a visit to London he attended the meeting of a fellowship of Christians at Lloyd's, the prominent marine insurance brokers, and shared his vision there. After the meeting someone came up to him and began telling him about a group called OM that had been praying for officers, crew and a ship for six years.

Bjørn immediately contacted the British captain for further information. He responded by offering Bjørn the position of first officer on a ship that did not yet exist. He then proceeded to enlist Bjørn's help in trying to find a suitable ship.

For a long time the British captain had been the only professional marine officer committed to the ship's project. In the eyes of most people he embodied the project—a captain without ship or crew. Then, in 1968, Bernhard Erne joined the project with his wife and baby son.

Bernhard had been at sea for a number of years when he became a Christian. Deciding that life at sea was not conducive to his spiritual growth, he returned to his home in Switzerland to work. Two years later he heard about the OM ship project and felt strongly that he should join it. His church could not understand his decision. Bernhard explained:

'Our church felt we were utterly crazy. "You're going to a movement you don't know," they said. "Those people are talking about ships but they don't know anything about them."

'One Sunday the pastor preached about Abraham and how he moved out in response to God's call. After the sermon I said to my pastor, "You see! You've just preached about how Abraham moved out because he believed."

' "Yes," said the pastor, "but *he* knew who called him."

'In spite of this, in 1968 we sold all our things and drove down to Belgium. The OM conference was at an old, empty brewery. From the letter we had received from OM beforehand we expected to find a ship's team meeting together and learning from each other. When we got to the brewery, we were told that we would be introduced to the ship's team. A man came in, a typical Englishman. It was the British captain. Later I met another man, but he left again. That was the entire ship's team!

'Afterwards we were told, "Now we will show you the place where you will stay."

'They took me to a building and showed me an empty room—absolutely barren, just four walls, the floor and the ceiling.

' "This is your room," they said, "We'll go and get something for you to lie on so you don't have to sleep on the floor."

'They went upstairs and one of them came back with a roll of corrugated cardboard under his arm. He put it on the floor and said, "OK, you can lie here."

' "Man," I thought, "what a crazy outfit!"

'I had a nice car, a Citroen, with reclining seats. I could have slept perfectly well there. But then I thought, "If I sleep in my car, they might think I am not so spiritual. I'd better go inside and sleep on the floor."

'That was my introduction to OM. If I hadn't sold everything, I think I would have returned home. But I believed God would provide the ship. That's why I stayed.'

After a year or so God began to bring in other men. Someone gave a pamphlet to someone else who sent it to someone in Australia. Eventually it landed in the hands of John Yarr, a chief engineer. So convinced was he that this was God's place of service for him that he left a well-paid job and brought his wife and four children to England in faith that the ship would soon materialise.

Other crew members began to come in: Rashad Babukhan, a young Arab deck officer from Aden, who had not even been a Christian at the time prayer for a ship began; Alfred Boschbach, a German cook who had just completed Bible college; Dave Thomas, a British engineer who had just recommitted his life to God after several years of indifference; and Decio de Carvalho, who left a good job with an international airline. By 1970 fifteen professional crew from ten different countries had joined.

For five years George Verwer and the British captain had been searching for a ship—not just any ship but one that would be suitable for OM's unique type of ministry. It must have a long range—that is, be able to travel long distances without stopping to refuel or take on water. It must have a lecture hall large enough for two or three hundred people. In addition, it must have space for a small book exhibition, storage and workshop area for vehicles, and accommodation facilities for at least a hundred and twenty crew and staff. Above all, it must be cheap. Eighty thousand pounds (about two hundred thousand dollars) was set as the upper limit.

Scores of ships were investigated but none seemed suitable. There was always some major drawback. Then in 1969 a friend in the shipping industry sent news to the British captain about a 2,625-ton ship, the *Zambesia*. A bit larger than was currently being contemplated, it nevertheless fell within the size range under consideration. All the data seemed right—adequate range, cabin space for sixty-five passengers plus crew, and adequate space to be converted into a meeting hall for three hundred people and into a maintenance base for vehicles.

Five years of praying and waiting and now this ship! Excitement began to grow and with it the feeling that God was finally answering. George Verwer published a leaflet called *Now is the hour for the ship*. He and the captain went to see the ship. The visit added to the escalating sense of expectancy.

Then came devastating news! The *Zambesia* had been sold to Nigerian buyers! The ship was gone, but the feeling of urgency remained, the conviction that God was about to do a big thing, not in the coming years but in the coming months or even weeks. That summer George had meetings with the other OM leaders, who expressed their conviction that the team should move into high gear in trying to secure a ship.

Impatient to see something happening, George dispatched two of his men to major shipping areas to see if they could uncover any possibilities. Peter Conlan, a twenty-five-year-old Englishman who had worked closely with George for three years in India and elsewhere, had just returned from the Keswick Convention in England when George said to him, 'Peter, I want you to go to Athens.'

'Whatever for?' asked Peter in surprise.

'I want you to look around and see if you can find a ship we might buy.'

With these words he thrust into Peter's hands the plane ticket and a book about Aristotle Onassis and how he got into shipping. Although Peter later confessed he had no idea what to do next, he nevertheless set off for Greece. In Athens he visited Onassis' private office. Onassis himself was in Paris, but Peter was able to talk to his managing director, who said, 'Look, if we gave you free the smallest ship we have on the market you couldn't cope with it.' It was massive.

George's other man was Mike Wiltshire, a young and gifted journalist who said he 'hardly knew one end of a ship from the other'. Mike was sent to scout out the shipyards in Scandinavia. As he visited shipyards and talked with shipping agents, one name kept recurring: the *Umanak*. The British captain and one or two others had already visited this Danish ship a few months earlier. They had rejected it as unsuitable, largely because its ventilation system, built for Greenland's climate, was totally inadequate for the heat of the tropics, and because it lacked a large auditorium.

But among the crew members who had come into the ship project by this time were several engineers. As they discussed among themselves the suitability of the *Umanak*, they became convinced it had strong possibilities. One of them, they decided, should go to George Verwer and present their ideas. George listened with great interest and decided to have a look for himself. Bjørn Kristiansen flew with him to Copenhagen to make the inspection. George had looked at many ships, but as he toured this one, for the first time he felt a deep conviction, 'This is it! This is the ship!'

There was a snag, however. A contract for its purchase had already been signed by Nigerian buyers, who had also put down a ten per cent deposit. The time limit for their payment had not elapsed, but they seemed to be encountering difficulty in producing the money or in getting it out of Nigeria. At any rate, there was nothing George or anyone else in OM could do except wait and pray. No doubt George recalled the words he had written after the *Zambesia* incident: 'The *Zambesia* was sold to Nigerian buyers before we could move into action . . . The temptation at times like this is to wish we had moved faster. Yet we are sure that the slow method is the more certain, for *no one else can get the ship the Lord has for us.*' (Much later someone heard that the new owners of the *Zambesia* had been plagued continually with problems with the tail shaft.)

Early in the summer of 1970, after four years of talking about the ship and working for it, the British captain had felt he should set a deadline for getting the vessel if he was to remain involved as captain.

If God had provided a ship with the contract signed by the end of August 1970, he would take that as a sign that he should remain in the project as captain. If God did not provide a ship by that time, he would withdraw from his position in the project.

His announcement came as a shock to many people. Some people felt as if someone who had been one of the very foundation stones of the project had suddenly decided to walk out. For other people the announcement only served to heighten the expectancy that God was going to bring in the ship soon, very soon, before the end of the summer.

Each autumn all OM workers in Europe would come together for a conference. For new OMers this was a time

of orientation and training to prepare them for the work
they would be doing. For people who had already been
with OM for a while it was a time of prayer, mutual
encouragement and planning of strategy.

In September of 1970 the conference was held in a cold,
draughty, disused factory in a suburb of London. One
morning George Verwer came rushing out of his office,
exploding with excitement, waving his arms in the air and
shouting at the top of his voice, 'Praise God! It's free! The
Umanak is free! The deal with the Nigerian buyers has
fallen through and the owners are ready to negotiate with
us!'

Others took up the cry. Within minutes everyone in the
building had heard the news. They were thunderstruck.
For years they had been praying and believing that God
would provide a ship. Once it had even seemed that the
ship was almost within grasp. Yet the whole idea still had
a vague, ethereal quality about it. The sudden announcement that the ship was a reality was too much to take in all
at once. But as the stunned minds started to function
again, little groups of two or three began to gather around
the building to discuss the new development, sometimes
in hushed, awed voices, sometimes in unrestrained enthusiasm. Spontaneously, the groups would break into
prayer, sometimes pleading with God to give them this
ship and sometimes simply committing the whole project
to God and asking that his will be done. Conference
meetings were begun with times of intense prayer about
the ship. Everyone's heart and mind were filled with one
topic: the ship. The feeling of excitement and anticipation
was so strong it was almost tangible. God was going to do
something great! Everyone was sure of it.

That very evening George Verwer left for Copenhagen
with Bjørn Kristiansen and John Yarr, the chief engineer,
to discuss terms with the owners, the Royal Greenland
Trading Company, which belonged to the Danish Government. The following morning they met briefly with the

owners before going out to inspect the ship again.
Arrangements were made for a marine engineer, a spe-
cialist, to go that afternoon to the ship to prepare a survey
report. The report, several pages long, indicated that OM
was 'getting a lot of ship'—and a good ship, at that—for
the money they were paying. Asked how many years he
thought OM could use the ship, which was built in 1949,
the surveyor estimated at least ten, perhaps more if the
vessel were well cared for.

The negotiations with the owners centred largely
around the attempt to get them to lower their price. But
they were adamant. The ship, which was originally
offered for £84,000, they would sell for £72,000. That was
the lowest figure. At this point George made a request.
Was there a small room somewhere that he could use to
talk to God about the matter? The owners were startled.
This was not the way they were accustomed to doing
business. But, of course, they did provide a room.

Finally the owners agreed to sell at £70,500 (about
$175,000) provided the decision to buy was made that
very evening, as other buyers were interested in the ship.
Immediately George got on the phone to contact the
necessary people, commenting to them with unmistakable
satisfaction that the owners had given him permission to
make international calls free of charge so that he could get
the agreement needed for this decision. The OM Boards
of Trustees in both the United States and Great Britain
were contacted. Other OM leaders were consulted,
including the British captain. All of them felt that the
price was reasonable and that George should proceed
with the negotiations for the purchase.

The following morning the terms of the contract were
discussed. A deposit of £7,000 was required. By the end
of September, less than three weeks away, seventy-five
per cent of the total cost must be paid. Fifteen days of
grace would then be allowed for the remaining twenty-five
per cent. Quite simple and straightforward. However, as

George later pointed out to OM people at the conference, they had been praying for the ship for over five years. In all that time only about £45,000 had been given. 'Now,' he said, 'we have only one month in which to come up with an additional £25,000. This means going on our knees and praying in the remaining amount of money. We have thrown ourselves out on the limb of faith, perhaps more than we ever have in the history of the work. If we do not come up with the money at the right time, it is almost certain that we will lose our deposit of £7,000. I don't believe that any of us could possibly conceive that it is the Lord's will for this deposit to be lost. This means that we must get on our faces before God, trusting him for the impossible.'

Along with prayer George was aware of his need for some sound practical advice in dealing with the legal aspects of the purchase. Val Grieve, a long-time supporter of OM, was contacted. As a lawyer working in the city of Manchester, in the north-west of England, he'd never dealt with the purchase of a ship, but he agreed to advise OM in the matter. Of his involvement he wrote:

'My advice was that a Company needed to be formed to own the ship. Also, in those days it was necessary to apply to the Bank of England for permission to send money abroad. I advised that we should apply for this as soon as possible. Rather to my amazement I was then elected Chairman of the Company [Educational Book Exhibits] with the responsibility of dealing with this purchase. The most unusual application which the Bank of England has ever received must have then been made. It was on behalf of a Company that wasn't formed to send money we hadn't got!

'When I got back to my office in Manchester I wondered what was happening. Many years of legal training had taught me that anyone who buys a house must, first of all, be certain about their mortgage arrangements so that the necessary monies were available on completion. I was now Chairman of a Company that had bought a ship by faith.'

As prayer for the ship continued during the conference, various people began to suggest names for the ship.

George Verwer, deciding that the time had come to make some decision about the name, passed out slips of paper at one of the conference meetings. Everyone was to write down suggestions for a name and then pass the paper up to George, who stood in front and read out the names as they came in. The audience listened attentively, sometimes making comments or offering a murmur of approval. Most of the suggestions were serious, but occasionally a flippant one turned up, such as *George's Folly*. A suggestion appearing several times was the name *Logos*, meaning 'word' in Greek and used in the Bible to refer to the Lord Jesus. No decision was made at the time, but a general sense of agreement began to grow that the name should be *Logos*.

The deadline for the final payment had been set for 15 October 1970. On the evening of 10 October a small group of crew members loaded their sleeping bags and suitcases into a van, said goodbye to friends at the conference and started off for Copenhagen. Decio de Carvalho, one of those crew members, wrote of that trip:

'It was a long trip filled with hopes and joy, fears and misgivings. We were about to take over a ship not yet ours in the name of a company that did not exist officially . . .

'We drove directly to the wharf in Copenhagen where the *Umanak* had been berthed for the last eighteen months. The orange-painted hu.. of the vessel now possessed only a trace of her former glory. But her figure and features were still impressive. Our group was strangely quiet in a mixture of awe and tiredness. Some of us tried a few breezy remarks to hide our emotions, but at the end we settled for the only thing our hearts could tell us to do on such a portentous occasion; we prayed. And even as we bowed our heads, we excused ourselves often from the Lord's presence to cast furtive, incredulous looks at our miracle ship—a mixture of faith, joy and apprehension in our hearts . . .

'On 13 October 1970 we moved on board as a group, having cleared with the owner our intention of staying on the vessel until the transfer of ownership was completed. We went in with our sleeping bags, sandwiches, brooms and mops, and we set out to work in faith, trusting that within two days' time the whole amount of the ship's agreed price would be in the joint bank account in the name of the owner and EBE. Yet the owner's representatives were not sure that we would ever make it. Whoever buys ships nowadays, paying a hundred per cent cash without any bank's financial aid, especially when the buyer openly confesses to having no other money at all when signing the purchase contract?'

Others had more mixed feelings. When the little group first sighted the ship, Captain Kristiansen kept saying, 'With a little paint she'll look lovely! Ah, she's a lovely ship! She's a lovely ship!' Putting his hands together, he rubbed them back and forth in his excitement.

'I didn't know what to expect,' said Olivia de Carvalho, the only woman in the group at that time. 'I remember going on board for the very first time and thinking, "Oh my word!" It was unbelievable! The previous crew had just walked off and left everything. I stepped into the engineers' mess and the plates were still on the table. There were fish bones in the plates and cigarette butts all over the place. It was really dirty!'

The galley was just as big a mess. While the men were doing other work, Olivia tackled the job of cleaning the galley.

'I spent two full days trying to clean it up,' she said. 'I could hardly lift the big pots and pans. They were so heavy. Finally I got the place clean and sat down in the engineers' mess with several of the men, exhausted from the work we had already done. All of a sudden bellowing, black smoke came rolling down the hall from the galley. John Yarr sprang from his chair, quick as a panther, and made a dive for the galley door.

'They had an oil stove, or whatever it was. I called it "the dragon". Something had gone wrong and it was belching out smoke. I stood there and cried. I had just spent two days cleaning that kitchen! When I went back everything was black. It was awful! I thought, "I'll never survive this ship." '

However, Olivia soon bounced back to her usual happy, optimistic self.

While all the cleaning and other work on the ship was being done, formalities for the purchase of the ship were carried out. Olivia's husband Decio was involved in these:

'In the morning of the fifteenth, George Verwer and Val Grieve arrived in Copenhagen. A few of us sat together around a desk in the office of the owner's executives. Our joint account, when examined, showed that we had deposited, from various sources, one thousand dollars more than the contractual price! We looked at each other, searching for the right reactions to show or the right words to say. The ship was ours! The unbelieving ship owners gasped, and we, the new owners, opened our hearts in praise to the Lord then and there. The documents of transfer of ownership were properly and solemnly signed by all parties. Then the sellers wanted to insist on the traditional toasting with best Scotch whisky, but finally settled for George's suggestion of an ice-cream cake.

'A few hours later our small group, some still in dirty clothes from their cleaning jobs, gathered together in the captain's cabin where George led us in a simple round of prayers, committing the ship to the Lord, now that she was officially "ours". And we praised him! Oh, how we praised him that day!'

3
God's ship

The ship was theirs! This was something that had to be celebrated, not with ice-cream cake, but in a much better way. Danish Christians who had heard of the purchase were invited to come and tour 'this amazing gift of the Lord' and participate in a service of dedication. A couple of hundred people gathered that day on the foredeck of the *Logos* and listened to George Verwer pour out his heart as he told them what God had done and what he was expecting God to do with the ship.

An older man who listened to George told him a strange story afterwards. He had been a missionary and had travelled on the ship when she was the *Umanak* carrying passengers between Greenland and Denmark. At one point he had become so troubled by the wild, drunken revelry; the loud, frantic but empty pursuit of pleasure, that he went below to his cabin and prayed for those people. That night he had a dream. The ship was a Christian one. Instead of having a boisterous and drunken party, the people were praying and singing praises to God. The captain was talking about his experience with God. That dream, the missionary realised, had now come true.

The story made a deep impression upon Bjørn

Kristiansen as he realised that *he* was the captain in the dream. *He* was the one who had been chosen to be captain of the Christian ship. In months ahead when difficult times came, this story was one of his sources of encouragement.

On 22 October the *Logos*, her new name boldly painted on the hull, set off for Rotterdam, where she would be overhauled. For eighteen months the *Umanak* had been 'dead', that is, out of use. 'Dead' is an apt description, for without the continuous drone of the generators and the bustling sound of people going about their work, a ship becomes unnaturally quiet and takes on an eerie atmosphere of unreality. In such a state it begins to deteriorate. After a year and a half of being 'dead', the *Umanak* required a great deal of overhauling. It also had a major problem in that the propellor shaft had been damaged. This could only be repaired in dry dock.

With a damaged propellor shaft and with her propellor sitting on deck, the *Logos* could not sail under her own power. She had to be towed to a dry dock. Arrangements were made with a German company that had a tug that had just been to Scandinavia. Since it had to return to Germany anyway, the owners offered a bargain price for towing the *Logos*.

When George Verwer and the other OM representatives had met the *Umanak* owners to discuss terms, they had stated to the sceptical owners their very firm conviction that God would provide the money to pay. When the final day of reckoning came, not only was the full amount at hand but there was money left over.

'Your God doesn't know accounting very well,' joked one of the men. 'I expected to see the exact amount.'

'Oh, you're wrong, sir,' replied Captain Kristiansen. 'Just before I came to this meeting I contracted for a tugboat. That "leftover" money was exactly what it cost to tow this ship down to Rotterdam.'

On the *Logos* in Copenhagen were not only crew but also two wives and one nine-year-old child. Olivia de

Carvalho tells one story which illustrates how the different senses of humour of different cultures could cause
problems:

'Bjørn Kristiansen had a way of teasing us. We never knew
whether he was serious or not and sometimes he would forget
to tell us. One morning at breakfast he said that the women
and children might not be able to travel with the ship to
Rotterdam, on her maiden voyage, because seamen believe
that women on board will bring bad luck.

'And he went on to say that we might have to go by train
and meet the ship in Rotterdam.

'Susanne absolutely fell apart. "It's ridiculous," she pro-
tested indignantly, "that a woman can't go across on the
maiden voyage. It's just some old sailors' nonsense. This is
God's ship! We're not superstitious."

'And she decided to take the whole thing into her own
hands.

' "Come on, Olivia," she said decisively. "We're going to
talk to that tugboat captain!"

'So we hopped across the wharf and jumped on board the
tugboat.

'The captain was surprised when we came bolting into his
cabin, and Susanne told him the whole story of what Bjørn
had said. He began to laugh, and assured us it was perfectly
all right. We could sail with our ship. His men would be even
more cautious and careful, knowing women and children
were on board. There certainly were no rules or regulations
about it.

'We came back triumphantly and told Bjørn. He hit the
roof! He said we had no business going to the tugboat captain.

' "I was only kidding you about the voyage," he said. And
then he had to put on his best suit and go over to talk with the
tugboat captain and try to explain this strange crew he had on
board.'

When it was time to sail, two steel cables from the tug
were attached to the *Logos*, one on either side. These
cables were so heavy and thick that one man alone could
not secure them. It took two or three men to bend, twist

and turn them around the thick, squat metal post called a bitt and fasten them securely. These preparations made, the tug with the *Logos* in tow was ready to set off on a trip that the skeleton crew aboard the *Logos* would never forget.

The problems began before the *Logos* left. The ship was continually listing to one side or the other. Like other ships, she had several ballast tanks to maintain stability. With the right balance in water levels in all the tanks she would stand upright and steady, without listing. Because the *Logos* was at a shallow berth, her tanks had been almost emptied to give her greater buoyancy. To be shifted to another berth, she needed the stability of these tanks once again.

The usual procedure on European ships is for the captain or chief officer to assign someone, usually the carpenter, to take soundings to measure the depth of the water in each tank. He reports his findings to the captain or chief officer, who then gives orders to the engineers to transfer water into or out of the tanks.

On the *Logos* there were a few hitches in the procedure. The system for filling the tanks was awkward. Most ships have one central filling pipe which branches off to each tank. The flow of water into each tank can be easily regulated through valves. The *Logos*, however, had no central filling pipe. Each tank had to be filled directly through a vent that opened onto the deck.

Then there was the problem of the carpenter assigned to measure the water in the tanks. An older seafaring man, he had got into conversation with several of the former *Umanak* crew and had been given considerable information about filling the ballast tanks. But, as he was a carpenter and not an officer, the deck and engineer officers were sceptical of the advice he passed on.

At one point the ship gave a sudden lurch, listing more heavily to one side than usual. Faces of the *Logos* crew registered shock and fear. People appeared at the windows of the office building on shore nearby, staring in amazement at the ship they had always known to be a stable, upright vessel.

The list was corrected as water was transferred to the proper tank. The listing, however, was only the symptom of a much deeper problem, which remained. The crew manning the *Logos* did not know one another and consequently did not trust one another. Many of them were new to OM and did not know what it was all about or how it operated. Some were not even clear about the purpose of the ship; they just knew it was to be used somehow for Christian work.

Up until recent times in nautical history the captain and his deck officers were supreme in authority and status on a ship. But with the invention of engine-powered ships another group of vitally necessary men came on the scene—the engineers. With each advance in the development of marine engines, the engineers took on greater importance until nowadays, on most ships, the chief engineer is considered almost equal to the captain in importance, though the captain is still ultimately responsible for his vessel. Salaries are similar, if not equal. Fully aware of their own vital role in running the ship, engineers sometimes become resentful of the fact that deck officers are traditionally afforded public respect and adulation while the engineers are often ignored. As a result, on almost every ship there is some degree of tension between engineers and deck officers, a tension expressed in a wide range of reactions from good-natured teasing to deep resentment and bitterness.

In addition to this tension, there is the natural tension that arises when people of different temperaments, outlooks and standards are forced to work closely together, particularly when they occupy positions of authority. The OM ship's project by its very nature tended to attract the bold, individualistic, adventurous types, so the OM ship had a superabundance of forceful, bigger-than-life personalities—the kind of people who have the vision and drive necessary to pioneer a project but who also, unfortunately, often produce a trail of sparks as they rub against others in the process.

The *Logos*, as she set off on her first voyage as 'God's ship', was to become a battlefield of personality conflicts.

Sailing on board as captain was Bjørn Kristiansen, the Norwegian captain who had so recently turned his life over to God. After much soul-searching and prayer, the British captain who had helped to spearhead the project had announced that he would withdraw as captain if the Lord had not provided a ship by the end of August. The call from the owners of the *Umanak* came on 8 September. Much pressure was put on the captain to reconsider. Inevitably people pointed out the fact that the timing was so close as to make little real difference.

'That's just the point,' he replied. 'If God had wanted me to sail as captain, he could easily have brought in the ship a couple of weeks earlier.'

Not many men could have poured themselves wholeheartedly into developing a project for five years and then withdrawn at the moment of fulfillment. God had used him in preparing the way for the *Logos*. Now he felt God was telling him to step aside from the limelight. Disregarding what others might think, he obeyed God.

He continued supporting the ship's project—he even served on its Board of Directors—but he never sailed as the ship's captain. Years later as he looked back over the way God had used the ship, he commented, 'I can see now why God did not want me on the ship as captain. If I'd been in authority, I would never have allowed the project to develop as it did.'

Bjørn Kristiansen took command of the vessel as it pulled out of Copenhagen that October morning. It was a job he had not wanted. He felt he was too young as a Christian to handle a responsibility like this. But there was no one else. Reluctantly he accepted the position, but he was very conscious of his need of God. When the ship family met together for devotions in the mornings, he would constantly remind the Lord that he had never been to sea with so many people who didn't know anything about sailing. He pleaded with God to watch over him, the people and the ship.

With him were seventeen officers and crew. Several of the crew had been trained in engineering, carpentry or some other practical skill on land, but had never been at sea. All of them—experienced seafarer or not—had given up well-paid jobs and come to serve God as unpaid volunteers on this ship. They were not preachers or theologians but they had a desire to use their practical knowledge and skills to make God known to people who needed him. Unfortunately, George Verwer returned to England to deal with other projects rather than sailing down to Rotterdam, leaving only mariners aboard with no one to give them the spiritual leadership that would be so sorely needed.

Even before the ship left Copenhagen, the power play had begun. Deck officers were pitted against the engineers. There was more to it, though, than just a struggle between deck and engineer officers. Different countries have different outlooks on nautical procedure, and the officers on the *Logos* reflected these differences. The British were well schooled in the tradition that everything should be done exactly according to properly-formulated and carefully-laid-out rules and regulations. Discipline, advance planning, and order were the keywords. The continentals were pragmatists. Getting the job done was more important than the process followed. Emphasis was on practical work rather than on the theoretical, and procedure was regarded in a much more relaxed way though safety rules were rigidly observed. Which perspective would gain precedence? That was the burning issue.

Because the *Logos* was in tow rather than steering herself, she could not go through the Kiel Canal, which would have been the shortest route. Instead she had to go up north around the tip of Denmark and then proceed south through the North Sea to Rotterdam. As she came around that northern part and entered the North Sea, she was suddenly plunged into a massive storm with Force Eight winds. The winds were so strong that they ripped to shreds the canvas surrounding the metal framework of the huge 'balloon' that must be hoisted aloft to indicate a ship in tow. Veteran seamen became grossly seasick, mindlessly forcing themselves to hang on till the end of their seemingly endless four-hour watches. Just watching the little tug pop up and down on the waves was enough to destroy the last vestige of self-control and precipitate a sudden rush for the rails at the side of the ship.

Ken Rotter, though an engineer, got a chance to try his hand at the wheel during the storm and described it as 'like a truck that had lost its shock absorbers and its steering mechanism.'

In the middle of all this violent movement of the sea, the horizontal shaft, which normally led to the propellor, came loose from the wires that had strapped it in place and began to roll back and forth on the rails supporting it, smashing violently against the pipes that lined the sides of the shaft tunnel. Ken Rotter was given the frightening job of crawling under the shaft as it careened wildly on the supporting rails, and fastening the wires in place again. It was with heartfelt relief that he saw the job successfully completed. Battered pipes bore mute testimony to that incident for the remainder of the ship's existence.

More trouble was yet to come. The thick, heavy steel cable fastening the *Logos* to the tug snapped in two like a flimsy piece of string. Re-securing the line in such storm conditions was no easy manoeuvre. Unfortunately, it was a job that had to be repeated, for the cable snapped several times. The tugboat captain couldn't understand it. Such a thing had never happened to him before. Captain Kristiansen was very uneasy. Tension heightened.

A man from the tugboat was transferred to the *Logos* to keep an eye on the lines. The tug came alongside and

he climbed up the rope ladder on the side of the *Logos*—
a risky venture, with both vessels lurching unpredictably
in the violently heaving waves. Coming aboard, the tugboat man found himself in what must have been a unique
situation for him. There were no cigarettes on board and
no alcohol. Even the supply of sugar ran out. And all
these strange people did was sing and pray.

The trip, which should have taken about two days,
stretched out to seven. Several people on board mentioned sensing the presence of evil so strongly that it was
almost tangible. It was as if the devil was digging in his
heels and making one last determined stand to try to
prevent the ship from passing into God's hands. Every
means at his disposal he seemed to pounce upon and twist
into his own weapon. The natural weaknesses of the men
were exploited to the full, resulting in quarrelling, complaining and criticism.

Decio de Carvalho, one of the crew without sea experience, said later:

> 'I saw from the very beginning that Satan was going to fight
> that ship to the end, that he was determined not to let it get to
> Rotterdam. One of the main things he used was people. That
> was when problems came to a head between the engineer and
> deck officers. It was more than just personality clashes, lack
> of sleep, temper, fear and seasickness. It was Satan pitting
> one man against another.
>
> 'Suddenly it dawned on me that someone had to take
> spiritual leadership and start fighting back. Of course, I was
> the wrong man for it. I had no experience in leading any-
> thing, especially a group like that. But I was desperate. All I
> could think of was to sit down and organise a prayer chain. I
> felt if two individuals were praying at all times, twenty-four
> hours a day, that would be the only way we could get the ship
> across.'

Many of the crew as well as the women took part in the
prayer chain. Others just simply prayed alone, quietly,
but desperately praying, not necessarily for spiritual victory but just for survival. When they met together for

morning devotions or at other times during the day, they would repeatedly sing one song that expressed their feelings and hopes, their confidence even when things looked dark:

> 'Glory to God, he has lifted me up,
> He has lifted me up, I know;
> For he reached out his hand, and he lifted me up,
> And that's why I love him so.'

All in all, it was indeed a memorable voyage.

'The tug-boat men must have heaved a sigh of relief when they'd got us to Rotterdam safe and sound,' said Olivia. 'The man who was on our ship really hated to go though. The tug crew would go back and forth between their boat and ours. They went back to theirs and got some sugar because we'd run out on the way down. They hated to leave us, but finally they had to go. They just blew their whistle loudly and waved and waved to us like we were something very, very special.'

4

Preparing to sail

In Rotterdam the crew began working feverishly to bring the ship back into working order. During the long lie-up in Copenhagen it had lost its 'classification' and needed to regain it. Bureau Veritas, the society which classified the ship, had many specific regulations governing the standards that must be met in areas like safety features, pollution control, the structure of the hull and the functioning of the machinery aboard. Only when these conditions were fully met and certified by a surveyor, would the ship be approved by Bureau Veritas and be considered classified. This was not a once-for-all event, for at certain specified intervals the ship would have to be checked again by a marine surveyor in order to retain classification. Without classification the ship would be denied entry to most ports of the world.

In Rotterdam, therefore, the crew faced the immense task of getting the ship up to standard. The main engines and generators needed to be overhauled. The huge three-ton propellor which had been carried to Rotterdam on deck had to be installed. All sorts of things had to be checked by a surveyor, from testing the water tightness of the portholes or the working order of the lifting gears, to inspecting the ballast tanks and assessing the stability of the vessel.

Another major task was installing an air-conditioning system to make the ship habitable in tropical climates. A tremendous amount of work needed to be done. While dock-yard workers did some of the major jobs, most of the work fell to the *Logos* crew. Every piece of machinery was taken apart and overhauled. That took time. The crew often worked far into the night, obsessed with the idea of trying to get the ship on its way as soon as possible.

The tensions and conflicts that had surfaced on the tow trip did not fade away when the ship reached Rotterdam. If anything, they intensified. Mistrust among the crew was a major problem. No one knew anyone else well, so no one had confidence in the abilities of others. Since they could not trust others to make correct decisions, many crew members tended to proceed with their work without consulting others.

Ebbo Buurma had never been at sea but he had worked for a number of years in a shipyard in Holland, where he was considered a skilled welder. Yet when he came on the *Logos*, he was not allowed to do the most simple welding job. He was not a seaman, so it was assumed he was not qualified. For example, the double bottom of one of the oil tanks was filled with rust holes which needed to be filled in by welding. Although it was one of the most elementary jobs in welding, Ebbo was not allowed to do it. Instead, someone from on shore was paid to come and do it. Ebbo was left feeling like a complete idiot, as he put it. 'Why did I come,' he asked himself, 'if this one little gift I have is not going to be used?'

It was an atmosphere like this that George Verwer entered as he returned to the ship in Rotterdam. But even he found himself out of his depth in this situation. His experience had been in challenging and leading young people in different forms of Christian ministry, but working with seafaring men who wanted to serve God with their practical skills, experienced men who had had to prove themselves in the hard and relentless rough-and-tumble of the working world—this was a completely new and frustrating situation for George. He could see what was happening to the ship's company, but when he tried to challenge them to love, unity and humility in relationships, his words often seemed to bounce off a brick wall. At times no one appeared to even hear them. At least, not the professional mariners.

These professional seamen and craftsmen, however, were only a small part of the ship's company, for in Rotterdam the non-crew members joined the ship. These included wives and children of the crew, plus young and unskilled men ready to work in any capacity, leaders in the ministry aspect of the ship, their families, secretaries, a bookkeeper, a teacher for the children and various other kinds of workers needed for the ship. Entire families were to live on the ship. No one was quite sure how this would all work out. Someone even suggested that all the children live and be cared for in a big nursery. That idea was quickly squelched.

Vera Buurma, wife of Ebbo, the welder, spoke of her experience as she first set foot on the ship that was to become her home for six years:

'I had no, no idea what I was going into. I was all excited so I phoned my husband, who was already working on the ship, and asked him, "What does a cabin look like?"

'He was rather quiet at the other end of the phone, which was very unusual for my husband. Then he said softly, "It's very small."

'At that point I started to get a little bit worried. Anyway, with great enthusiasm I packed my bags. And I didn't pack just my bags. I packed two VW vans as well. I'm a Dutch person and Dutch people like to have their homes nice and cosy. I thought, you know, this would be really nice to take along—a little basket here for some newspapers, a little something there. So I came on the ship with a six-week-old baby and two vans loaded full of stuff. We went up the gangway and to our cabin. My husband opened the door and I got a shock! I couldn't believe that this was happening! Two beds, one above the other, and a little couch hardly big enough to hold the baby, a little table and a chair. That was it. There was no room for anything else, no room at all. We just sent our stuff back immediately. Actually it's amazing what the human mind can achieve because after a year I thought it was quite comfortable and the cabin looked quite big.'

Accommodation on the ship was so tight that it was easy not to appreciate the needs of other people on board. Often, this was not due to selfishness, just a lack of understanding. In Rotterdam, the man in charge of the electronics department came aboard with all kinds of wires and gadgets. He went roaming through the ship looking in every nook and cranny for places to store all his equipment. A little cabin way up in the bow of the ship struck him as ideal. A good part of his stuff went into that room.

When the time came for single women to join the ship, Olivia and several others went through the ship deciding which cabins should be assigned to which people. The little cabin in the bow was assigned to a young woman named Phyllis. Olivia informed the electronics man that the cabin would be required for accommodation.

'Who's going to have the cabin?' he asked.

Olivia told him.

'OK,' he said.

A couple of days later Olivia went back to check on the cabin. All the wires and other things were still there.

'Oh no,' thought Olivia. 'What do I do now?'

Her face must have reflected her perplexity because when she met Drena Verwer, George's wife, in the alleyway, Drena asked, 'What's the matter? You look disturbed.'

'Yes,' replied Olivia, 'I told our electronics man we needed this cabin in the bow of the ship for Phyllis. He has a lot of equipment in there. When I asked him about it, he just told me that Phyllis was a good old soldier. She would understand.'

'Good old soldier or not,' declared Drena indignantly, 'she's a woman and she wants her cupboards!'

Off Drena marched to do something about the situation. The next time Olivia looked into the cabin, all the equipment was gone. Phyllis, who knew nothing of this interplay, arrived to find an empty cabin waiting for her.

Not only did the presence of women on board require some adjustment and understanding on the part of the male workers on the *Logos*, it was also something completely outside the experience of the shipyard workers in Rotterdam.

'The first night we got to Rotterdam and got the ship "parked" and so forth, we all went off,' said Olivia. 'We couldn't wait to get off and go walking around. Decio and I walked the streets and looked at the shops and just had a good time. We came back to get on the ship and the man wouldn't let me in the gate. It took a long time and many phone calls for this man to get it through his head that I could go on that ship, that it was my ship and I belonged there. He kept telling us, "No women on board! No women on board!" I kept trying to tell him that's where I lived.'

'I can remember Bernhard Erne laughing his head off. He thought that was the funniest thing that had happened in a long time.'

During the dry dock all the women had to leave the ship and stay in accommodation ashore. Just before Christmas the *Logos* came out of dry dock and berthed again at the quayside. Next to her lay a Dutch submarine. As the *Logos* women all marched past the submarine to return to the ship, 'the poor man on watch on the submarine,' observed Olivia, 'didn't know whether to whistle or to shoot or simply to look the other way!'

While the crew were trying to get the ship into shape, the non-crew members were occupied in evangelism. With great enthusiasm they set out into town to talk with people about the Lord Jesus Christ. Ebbo Buurma remembers his experience while strolling with George Verwer along the main pedestrian walkway in the town. 'Suddenly George got an urge to preach in the street,' he

said, 'and he grabbed me to translate.' Teams went out in
the evenings and weekends to visit various churches, sharing their testimonies and telling people about the ship.
Other teams travelled into the surrounding countries. In
addition, people came to the ship for tours and meetings,
which were held in the small lounge or dining-room. In
the evening crew members would often visit other ships in
the harbour, looking for opportunities to talk to the crews
from these ships and to share with them their experiences
with Jesus Christ.

The *Logos* people were overwhelmed by the loving
generosity of local Christians. For the entire three-month
stay of the *Logos* in Rotterdam the ship was supplied each
day with thirty loaves of bread from a local baker. A local
laundry did all the laundry for the ship people free of
charge. The owner of a battery factory donated a four-
year supply of car batteries. Other people gave dishes,
clothes, rope, and other equipment. The Philips Company of Holland provided a closed-circuit television system at below cost price.

A number of experienced shipping men took extended
leave to come and help. Other non-professional people
volunteered their services in any way they could be of use.
There continued to be a highly-charged atmosphere of
expectation that God was going to do something great,
and a growing sense of exhilaration in being involved in
what God was doing.

Few internal changes were made to adapt the ship to
the specific needs of OM. People were too uncertain
about the future role of the ship to be able to visualise
what changes might be needed. The main idea was that
the ship would be used to transport Christian workers
from port to port, where they would be involved in evangelism. The thought was that the ship would come into a
port and disgorge its workers to do the same sort of things
OM was doing on its land-based teams—distribute tracts,
sell literature door-to-door, hold open-air meetings, show

gospel films, speak in churches and try to get the people there involved in different forms of evangelism.

There would be meetings on board as well. For example, conferences could be held for local pastors. Of course, there was no auditorium on the ship, but the dining-room, which could probably hold up to eighty or ninety people, would undoubtedly provide adequate facilities for this.

When the ship reached India, its final destination, nationals could be brought aboard for several weeks of training, getting teaching during the voyages and practical training in evangelism in port.

Finally, book exhibitions were planned. Many people saw this more as a 'front' than as a real ministry. A ship bringing educational books to a needy country had a legitimate reason for being there—a reason non-Christian government officials would recognise. So some place had to be found to display these books, but it should not need too much space. Then, too, there were the Christian books. While some of these might be sold to pastors at conferences or to other visitors, most of them would probably be sold by ship's people who went ashore to do evangelism or to speak in church meetings. Different ideas were proposed for the location of the book exhibit, but as it was not a priority item, nothing was actually done.

While the crew was busy on the ship in Rotterdam, other people in London were trying to get the ship registered. The British company called Educational Book Exhibits had been formed to direct the affairs of the ship and to take legal responsibility for it. After much discussion the Board of Directors of this company decided that the ship should be registered in a neutral country, one that would not cause any political questions to be raised when the ship came into port. They chose Singapore, and contacted the Singapore Trade Commission in London.

On 24 December 1970, Peter Conlan flew to Singapore to try to get the ship registered. There, the big problem he faced was how the ship should be classified—as a cargo vessel or what? The *Logos* was unique, there was no precedent to follow. Officials were baffled. Finally they concluded they could not offer the classification Peter was seeking. In disappointment Peter left Singapore for East Pakistan, where he was scheduled to speak in some meetings. But there he began to wonder if it would not be worth another try. He sent a telegram to the man with whom he had stayed in Singapore; Russell Self, head of the Bible Society there, requesting him to make a few enquiries and asking whether it would be worthwhile to return. The reply came promptly: 'God is in this. Come back again. Let's see what we can do.'

Peter returned to Singapore and spent a whole day with an expert from the Singapore marine department, going through legal books trying to find some slot into which *Logos* could legally fit. Peter himself understood almost nothing of international marine law, but enthusiastically urged the expert to persevere in his search and prayed for a miracle. To their relief, a slot was finally found. Within twenty-four hours the *Logos* was registered as a Singaporean ship.

Back in Rotterdam the crew, deeply conscious of the momentousness of the occasion, welded the name *Logos* on the side of the ship.

The single event that stands out most in the minds of the people who were on the *Logos* in Rotterdam was the time the ship almost capsized. Ebbo Buurma, the Dutch welder, tells the story:

'There was a difference of opinion on how to handle the ballast on the ship. One day some of the men had pumped a couple of tanks empty and the ship made a slight list. We were told to fill up the tanks again with water. I was giving a hand with the filling up, together with Bernhard Erne, the bos'un. As we were standing on the foredeck, we saw the ship make a slight starboard list and then come up straight. But she didn't stop when she got up straight; she just kept moving on with sudden incredible speed to an extreme list on the port side till the ship practically dropped on the quayside. Bernhard reacted instantly, screaming, "Get the wives and children off!" A Dutchman who was on the ship to fill it up with water, a man who had been his whole life loading water on ships in the Rotterdam harbour, jumped straight from the ship onto the quayside because he was dead scared the whole ship would turn over. I rushed into the ship and had to walk up a slope of almost thirty-five degrees and I had to push up on the door of my cabin in order to get in. There I saw my wife Vera in the cabin with our son Stefan, totally undisturbed by this slight problem. She was just standing there, cleaning the top of the table.

' "Get off this ship!" I shouted.

' "What for?" she asked blankly.

' "Man, the whole ship is turning over!"

' "Oh," she said, "I thought that was normal."

'So we grabbed Stefan, who was only a few weeks old, and rushed on shore.'

George Verwer, who was standing on the shore with his little black briefcase in his hand, immediately dropped to his knees on the quayside, shouting hoarsely, 'Let's pray! Let's pray!' Captain Kristiansen was just returning from the post office where he had gone to make a phone call; he stopped abruptly and exclaimed in utter disbelief, 'What has happened to my ship?'

Everyone was rushed off the ship as quickly as possible, with crew members going through the ship to make sure everyone was off. Bernhard Erne remembered that one of the engineers who did night shift was asleep in his cabin. Dashing to the cabin, he turned the handle of the door and pushed strongly. Nothing happened; the door wouldn't budge. The tipping of the ship had made a drawer slide out of the dresser and become wedged against the door. Bernhard pounded loudly on the door until the engineer woke up.

In contrast to almost everyone else aboard, Chief Engineer Yarr displayed an air of confidence that all was under control. Dutifully having ordered everyone else ashore, he continued with what he had been doing when all the trouble started—frying eggs and bacon and making toast in the galley. Obviously in his element, he proceeded to hand out sandwiches to the ship people standing on the quayside in the biting wind.

Several hours' work were needed to return the ship to a stable, upright position. The accident was traced back to a lack of communication between departments. One department had emptied tanks so they could be steam-cleaned by a boat which had come alongside. Another department had ordered a supply of fresh water to be loaded from ashore. The unco-ordinated result was that the ship was thrown off balance. Captain Kristiansen was very upset because he had given strict instructions that the tanks should never be filled in the way they were that day. For several days the wives and children stayed ashore in the seamen's mission till everyone was sure the ship was completely safe.

Dave Thomas, one of the engineers, estimated the list at twenty-one degrees, saying that the ship had gone against the quayside and could have gone no further, so there was no danger of a capsize. Others, however, were not so sure. The fear that had been created in their minds was not to be erased quickly. For months afterward many of them kept a short length of string dangling in their cabins, a kind of plumbline to be checked out whenever the ship began to list.

The effects of the incident were not all negative. George Verwer felt that people were more ready to listen to him. Several of the officers met with him in the captain's cabin, where they discussed the situation and ended by kneeling down and asking God for forgiveness and help. Tensions between the crew members relaxed—for the time being.

5

Maiden voyage

In the early hours of 18 February the *Logos* moved slowly up the River Thames toward London after a smooth voyage from Rotterdam, the first voyage under her own power. In spite of the early hour, 3.00 a.m., many of the *Logos* people, keyed up with excited anticipation, were out on deck straining to make out the outline of the famous Tower Bridge as they drew near. To their surprise and delight, the sound of singing floated across the river. A group of Christians who had prayed for the ship for six years was standing on one of the towers of the bridge. As the ship passed under the bridge, they sang, 'To God be the glory; great things he has done.'

George Hider, of the London City Mission, remembers:

'I well remember getting a phone call early on Sunday morning saying "*Logos* will arrive in the pool of London in the early hours of Sunday." With my very young son in the car we drove up to Tower Bridge and positioned ourselves on the warship *Belfast* (whilst waiting he had the privilege of raising the flag on *Belfast*!)

'I still have the photo on my office notice-board to this day of the beautiful sight of *Logos* coming through Tower Bridge . . . the bridge having been raised, and the sun rising behind it. The day we had planned and prayed about had at long last arrived.'

A postal strike had paralysed much of the communication throughout Britain, leaving OMers wondering how many people would come to visit the *Logos*, for her first programme. They need not have worried. British OM teams had done an excellent job of getting the word out to interested Christians all over the country, many of whom had long prayed for the ship and were eager to see the reality of their prayers.

On the first Saturday the *Logos* was opened to the public some 1,600 people came aboard; not all at once, fortunately, but spread out throughout the day. Some of them came for scheduled meetings; a reception for Christian booksellers, a luncheon for leaders of various Christian missions, a meeting for students, a tea for ex-OMers. Others came simply to see the ship and were offered an extensive tour through most of the inner regions, viewing such things as the engine room, the large storage spaces called holds, the galley where all meals were prepared, the radio room, and the tiny cabins often providing accommodation for as many as four people.

One woman visiting the ship confided to a *Logos* person that she'd been about ready to give up on her marriage and perhaps on her Christian faith as well. But seeing the ship had made her realise that if God could provide a ship, he could certainly take care of her situation. She left the ship with a fresh commitment to her marriage and to God.

The day came to its climax at the Metropolitan Tabernacle, where more than a thousand people had crowded into the auditorium to hear the testimonies of Captain Kristiansen and Chief Engineer Yarr, a report about the ship and a brief challenge to which a number of people responded by re-dedicating their lives to Jesus Christ. At the end of the day the *Logos* people were exhausted yet happily content that their 'open house' had been a success and confident that people who had actually seen the ship would pray much more intelligently for its ministry.

Sunday and Monday, the two remaining days, were spent in similar hectic fashion, with Sunday dinner an occasion to meet the parents and pastors of British OMers and help them understand better what their young people were doing. Tuesday morning was spent in preparation for sailing later that day.

All of this activity was, of course, new and exhilarating for the young people on the *Logos*. Occasionally, though, there were experiences which were new but not exhilarating. One of the women who lived in a cabin in the bow of the ship was startled to wakefulness one night by an awful noise. The anchor was being let down, just on the other side of the bulkhead. The sound was horrific. Convinced that the ship had hit something, she grabbed her raincoat and life-jacket, struggling to put them on over her pyjamas as she rushed up to her lifeboat station. No one was there except Captain Kristiansen, one of the officers and a pilot. Captain Kristiansen looked at her enquiringly and said, 'Yes?'

Feeling like a fool the young woman returned to her cabin. Her embarrassment was not so much at what she had done as at what she had not done. She had forgotten to wake up her roommate when she dashed off to escape the 'catastrophe'.

The programme in London, however, was only a part of the ship activity that was going on and had been going on in Britain. Much of it was work behind the scenes.

Mike Wiltshire had been busy in Britain for many weeks. He was the first of many 'line-up' men, that is, men who would be sent to a port ahead of the ship to schedule (line up) meetings, plan the programme and make whatever arrangements were necessary in the port area. With absolutely no training or experience in this area, Mike, a journalist, had to feel his own way. What kind of arrangements were necessary for a ship like the

Logos to sail into London with its crew and staff carrying passports from more than a dozen countries?

Obviously some kind of arrangements had to be made with the port authorities in order to be able to dock in the port. Mike found the top man of the London Port Authority, Commander P F C Satow, to be extremely helpful, not only offering the ideal place to berth but offering it free of charge except for a very slight fee for use of such items as the buoys at the pier.

There was only one problem. The *Logos* was a large ship for that part of the Thames. The minimum depth of the water at the pier was charted at fourteen feet with high tide raising it to eighteen feet. Would that be enough for the *Logos*? Mike was not sure, as he'd heard from Captain Kristiansen that the draught of the ship (the part of the ship extending down under the water) would probably be sixteen to eighteen feet. The draught, of course, varies somewhat depending upon how heavily a ship is loaded. Clearly Mike with his inexperience needed more precise information to make a decision. Commander Satow added the additional information that, though the depth of the river was only fourteen feet, the river bed was very soft mud and an ice-strength vessel like the *Logos* ought to be able to sit in a foot of mud as other ships had done. Mike sent an urgent plea to Captain Kristiansen in Rotterdam for further guidance. Eventually the two decided the situation was workable.

Taking care of the technical aspects for docking the ship, and making arrangements for clearing the people aboard through customs and immigration authorities, was only part of the job the line-up man faced. The programme had to be planned as well. Working with OMers and other Christian leaders in the area, Mike had to decide what sort of groups of people should be invited on board for meetings or for meals, what kind of meetings could be held on shore and how ship personnel could get involved in Christian meetings already scheduled in churches and other places.

Arranging for the ship to come to Britain was going quite easily, Mike realised. After all, the *Logos* was technically owned by a British company. The Christian public was informed to some extent about the ship. And authorities tended to be sympathetic toward something religious. But what would happen when the ship tried to enter a country that had never heard of her? A ship that was neither cargo ship nor tourist ship, a ship that wanted to occupy a berth not just for a few hours or a couple of days like most ships but many days and perhaps even weeks, a ship full of people whose driving passion was to be able to talk to people about Jesus Christy—or, at least, to be able to give printed material that talked about him. How do you convince government officials in Africa or Asia that they want such a ship to visit their countries?

Mike had long before come to the conclusion that something had to be prepared which would present the *Logos* in an acceptable way. For six months he had been working on a brochure which he entitled *Educational Book Exhibit: Great Discoveries*. The big, glossy eight-page brochure presented the educational aspect of the ship in glowing terms, liberally interspersing the text with photos to add interest and credibility. It was quite an impressive presentation for a book exhibition which had never even taken place. In fact, the photos of the educational book exhibits were authentic. The name Educational Book Exhibit had been borrowed from an existing operation of OM, a team that had been moving around in India and Nepal using a large selection of educational books interspersed with a few Christian ones as a point of entry and interest in various towns and cities. Mike presented the *Logos* as providing 'a vital extension to the international Educational Book Exhibit programme of training, learning and education'.

While Mike Wiltshire was working on his glossy brochure, Philip Morris, an English OMer in his mid-twenties, was

finding great satisfaction in working with the original Educational Book Exhibits in India and Nepal. Shortly after
the purchase of the *Logos*, Philip received a letter from
George Verwer asking if he would come to England and
buy books for the exhibition on *Logos*.

'No,' wrote Philip in reply, 'I'm really enjoying my
work here.'

A telegram arrived saying in essence: 'Do as you're
told. Come.'

Philip got on a plane and went, arriving in Rotterdam
just after the ship. On board, he discovered that no one
had given any thought at all to where the book exhibition
was to go. Everyone was busy with his own work in
getting the ship repaired. Finally Philip managed to find
some people to discuss the problem, and together they
toured the ship and looked at the possibilities.

One choice would have been to use one of the holds—a
large, dark room below deck made for storing cargo. A
spiral staircase could be built for people to descend into
the hold. Proper lighting would have to be installed. The
problem was the possibility of a bottleneck if too many
people should visit the book exhibition at the same time.
Also, if there were a fire, how would all the people get
out?

Another idea was to use the dining-room. Someone
came up with the ingenious suggestion of making displays
which could be set on the tables but which would be
attached to pulleys. When the tables were needed for
meals, the displays could be pulled up to the ceiling. Not
surprisingly, this idea was discarded as impractical.

With the matter still undecided, Philip had to leave for
England to buy books. He said later:

> 'Nobody knew what sort of books we wanted. All we knew
> was that we wanted books for Africa and India. We thought
> we would probably want some books by authors from these
> places, but we really didn't have any more idea than that
> except we knew we wanted educational books. I got the

"yellow pages" from the London telephone directory and wrote to all the book companies listed there—about 170 or possibly even as many as 200. Then we had no word processors, no computers, so all the letters had to be typed personally to each of these companies. Along with the letters we sent a brochure of the ship. The letter just said basically, "We have bought a ship. We are going to be sailing to Africa and India and we want to buy some books. Can you send us your catalogues and we'll contact you for an interview?" The brochure gave only very general information about the ship. It had some pictures of a ship, but not even our ship because when the brochure was done we didn't have the ship. It just said that we would be having educational books and that we would be doing relief work. Intended for use in England with secular companies, it didn't give the slightest impression we were Christian. I think it just said that we believed in God or something very general like that. It had to be very general because when it was prepared we really had no idea what we were doing.

'So I sent the letters to these companies and over the next couple of weeks no more than twenty of them replied. Of those who did reply, there were several that looked promising. One of them was Hodder and Stoughton, which was one of the larger educational and, as it happened, religious book companies in Britain. We were only interested in the educational side though. I made an appointment to see the export sales manager.

'I went in and gave him my presentation, showed him the brochure (which he'd already got anyway), and told him that we wanted to buy books for the ship. He questioned me a little bit about the kind of books.

' "Well, I really don't know," I said, "but I'll take your advice."

'His next question was how we were going to pay for them; if we were going to pay cash.

' "Well, no," I answered, "we don't have cash, but we'd like some credit."

'I was terribly sincere and I think this must have come out because he asked me to wait a minute. He went off for about ten minutes and when he returned, he said, "The chairman of our company is in today. I just told him briefly about this and he'd like to see you."

'I was ushered into a room and there was the chairman of the company sitting behind a big desk. He asked me a few questions and I gave my little presentation again. That took all of two minutes; there was really not all that much to say.

'Then he asked me, "Philip, do you have trade references?"

'I didn't know what trade references were, so I hesitated. Then I stammered out, "Well, I'm not sure." Of course, now that I know what trade references are, I realise that I was telling him no. But I didn't know that then.

'Then he asked me about our bank account and whether we would pay by cash. So I explained again:

' "Actually, we live by faith and we believe that God will provide the money. However, where the books are concerned, as we sell the books, we will send the money back to pay for the books and then we'll order more."

'Then he explained to me what a trade reference was. "Philip," he said, "when you go to a company, if you're not paying cash, you can get the books on credit but people want a reference from you to know that you are in good standing with some company."

'Then he did an amazing thing. He said to me, "Philip, I really believe that this project is going to be a success. When you go around to other companies and they ask if you have a trade reference," and putting his hand into his pocket, he pulled out his card and handed it to me, "you tell them to phone me personally. I will give them a reference on your behalf."

'I could only think that this was a miracle from God. Years later I learned that after this meeting a handwritten note was sent from the chairman to the sales manager instructing him to give Educational Book Exhibits the very best discounts, the maximum payment terms and no pressure to pay.

'Of course, then, when I went to visit other companies after that, I just gave them his name and we got the best possible prices and terms everywhere.'

The launching of the ship project was covered very well in the Christian media in Britain. An editorial in one

Christian newspaper began with the words: 'It makes a refreshing change to turn from news of hard-up missions, theological college closure, protracted church reunion discussions and declining numbers, to a Christian project which, by its sheer audacity, takes one's breath away.'

Most of the publicity was favourable, but some people raised serious questions. James Sutton had several penetrating ones. Would the book exhibition be in competition with local Christian bookshops in various ports, thus hurting them? Was a training programme on a ship superior to one on land using already existing facilities? Was OM being realistic when it claimed that the ship would save large amounts of money by transporting people, vehicles and supplies to Asia? Had OM thought through the implications of their plans for relief work? Would they be willing to stop suddenly in the middle of a programme and dash off to some area of crisis?

The questions were valid ones deserving careful consideration, but at this point the *Logos* people had no final answers. Only time and experience could give them.

Long before these articles appeared, David Winter had written about the *Logos* in the Christian magazine *Crusade*. The ship project he referred to as a 'Gospel Blimp'. The term came from a fictional book in which some Christians evaded their day-to-day responsibility to their neighbours by devising a grandiose evangelistic scheme using a blimp—a costly spectacle devoid of any intrinsic value. One result of this article in *Crusade* was expressed in a letter written personally to George Verwer by an elderly Englishman named Norman Green:

'Ocean liners have always fascinated me from small boyhood and they still do (I'm 75 now) but what stung me into prayer action about "the ship" was that somewhat cynical and discourteous article in *Crusade* some months ago about the "Gospel Blimp". I just felt that if this vision is of the Lord we must pray the devil out of this attack and make the project a matter of praise and glory to HIM only. My wife and I are at

one in this and as he gives us grace, we will go on praying . . .'

With the passage of time and the acquisition of more
information about the ship project, David Winter revised
his opinion. While the ship was in London, he visited it
and had the opportunity to talk with various people on the
ship. After the visit this delightful paragraph appeared in
Crusade:

> 'I couldn't really have blamed them if they'd made me walk
> the plank into the murky and polluted waters of London
> docks, but in fact the crew of the good ship *Logos* summoned
> up all their reserves of Christian grace and welcomed me on
> board to inspect her and enjoy an excellent lunch in the ship's
> dining-room before she set sail to Asia. New readers won't
> know that last year I hastily and imprudently described this
> floating evangelistic centre of Operation Mobilisation as a
> "Gospel Blimp", but all this was kindly overlooked as dir-
> ector George Verwer showed me the wonders of this beau-
> tifully equipped vessel. All the facts are on page 30, but let
> me say here and now that this looks a well-planned, strategic
> and timely project, and that the people involved, well aware
> of the danger of this sort of thing, have got their feet firmly on
> the ground (or the deck, at any rate).'

While the *Logos* was in London, the Christian press
along with many other Christian leaders were invited to
the ship. During the visit they were given a tour of the
ship with an enthusiastic rundown of plans for the future.
As Mike Wiltshire stood with these people on the bridge,
he noticed one of the men turn to another and remark in a
loud stage whisper, 'I'll give the project one year!'

6

Passage to India

On 26 February, 1971, the *Logos* set sail from Britain on her first voyage to India. People on board were keyed up to a high pitch. Their goal for so many years was finally being realised. They were actually sailing! All the publicity they had received in Britain and the support and good wishes of so many Christian friends had added to the heightened sense of excitement.

The first ports of call were La Havre, in France, and Vigo, in Spain. As the *Logos* came into Vigo, she was first sighted by a local Christian who was enjoying a siesta in a spot overlooking the bay. Through his binoculars he was able to read the name *Logos*.

The next day over a hundred Christian leaders came from all over Spain for a three-day conference on the ship. One emphasis of the conference was prayer. Deeply concerned himself about the needs of India and other countries, George Verwer vividly presented these needs to the Christian leaders present and challenged them to pray both then and later. Several people commented that the idea of praying for other groups and for other nations had never occurred to them before.

In the main session George spoke to them about what he considered to be the four great needs of the church:

quiet listening to the voice of God; prayer and worship; unity and love; and reality instead of religious masquerading. It was a powerful message and many people were deeply stirred. This was evident the next morning as one could sense a deep spiritual bond between these Christians from different denominations and theological persuasions. Some deep divisions that were known to exist among several of the men began to heal.

While the conference was going on, other ship people were involved in different forms of evangelism. About six weeks after the Vigo visit a *Logos* couple received this letter:

'Dear Larry and Nancy:
'I'm the sailor you met in front of the telephone's centre in Vigo about two months ago. I accepted your kind invitation and got into the *Logos* ship with other sailors. Do you remember?

'Excuse me but I can't express my ideas too well in English than in Spanish, but I think you'll understand me.

'When I was in the *Logos* I realised that there was something strange in the air, all reminded me of Christ. I thought that the truth was in the Bible, but I didn't want to accept it.

'Some days later I went to Barcelona to pass an exam and there I visited an evangelist chapel. When I came back to Vigo, I went to visit a chapel here. The third time I visited the chapel I realised, for the first time in my life, that Christ was expecting to get into my life, but I never had opened the door of my heart. Then, after requesting mercy of my faults to him, I accepted Christ.

'Afterwards I felt a complete and new peace inside me. I was changed. I was a new man. It's true, and I think there are not words enough to explain my conversion, but Christ has changed and is changing my life . . .'

Before the *Logos* could leave Vigo, the shipping agent had to be paid. The captain had no cash to pay the bill and the agent refused to take an American cheque from a bank in Chicago that he knew nothing about. As the two men sat in the captain's cabin deliberating about what to do to break the impasse, someone knocked on the door.

'Come in,' called out Bjørn.

In walked a young woman who was serving as radio officer on a Norwegian ship tied up alongside the *Logos*.

'Our crew enjoyed our visit to your ship last evening very much and we'd like to give you a little gift which we have collected,' she explained as she handed an envelope to the captain.

Bjørn thanked her warmly. After she had left, he opened the envelope. Inside was the exact amount of money required for the agent.

Amazed, the agent said, 'Oh, keep the cash. You can give me the American cheque.'

The next port of call for the *Logos* was Las Palmas in the Canary Islands. This stop had been included in the itinerary for one main reason: to take on fuel. The *Logos* had left London with just enough fuel to get her to the Canary Islands, where fuel was much cheaper—about £12 a ton at that time. Only a short stopover was planned so no one had gone ahead to inform people about the ship or to plan a programme. As the *Logos* moved into the harbour, scores of her people stood on deck, leaning on the rails and eagerly drinking in all the new sights and impressions. To their surprise, several people stood on the quayside to welcome them. How had these people learned about the visit of the *Logos*? Unknown to the *Logos* people, the anticipated arrival of the ship had been featured on Spanish radio as the major news item of the day!

As soon as the ship was cleared for boarding, the welcoming committee, who turned out to be local Christians, came on the ship and were soon involved with the programme leaders in discussing plans for evangelism and meetings for the weekend. They also joined the ship family in their long time of prayer that evening.

After a busy weekend, the *Logos* moved out to anchor. The fuel had been taken aboard, but George Verwer and the other OM leaders had decided that the ship should not leave Europe until all the outstanding bills had been paid. The one for fuel was the major one. The people on board knew that there was no money. They had hoped it would come in while the *Logos* was in England. Christians there, as they saw the ship and understood the ministry, would surely respond by giving generously. This was a false assumption. Many British Christians felt that, if the OMers had needed money, they would have asked for it. But OM leaders at that time felt that they should not ask for money, nor even give any hint of financial need. If God was really in the work, they reasoned, he could do the prompting himself so that people would give.

The halt in the Canaries, then, was more than just a pause to wait for money to pay bills. It was a test to make sure that God was really in the project. If he was, he would provide. If he didn't provide, there was no point in trying to press on without him.

While they were at anchor, George called the *Logos* people together in the dining-room and said to them, 'I believe that God has stopped us in the most out-of-the-way place imaginable. Hardly anyone knows we are here. I believe God has done this because it's *his* ship and *he* wants the glory. We've gone out with a blaze of publicity and it's very easy for us to think, "Look at all we've done", when actually it's God who has done it.'

George went on to review the situation. 'God can't bless us,' he said, 'if our hearts are not right with him. There's been jealousy, complaining, squabbling and just lack of love generally among all of us here on board. We need to repent and confess these things to God. Only then can we expect him to answer our prayers for finance.'

That hit some people quite hard. They were very much aware of ways they had hurt one another. Deeply convicted, many of them went to one another and to God asking for forgiveness. Then they turned to God with confidence yet humility, asking him to supply the needed money. They were well aware of the fact that, apart from the people in the home offices, no one knew they were still there; the Christian public assumed they were on their way to Nigeria. Nobody knew of their great need. There was no one but God to help them.

Each day George would walk down the gangway on the side of the ship and step into a little launch that would take him ashore. There he would phone the home offices to see if the money had come in. Each day he returned with disappointing news. The ship family continued waiting and praying. Ebbo Buurma remembers thinking, 'Dear me, we have hardly started and the money is finished already. How is this going to continue?'

Not all the time was spent in prayer. Work on the ship had to continue. The ship had to be kept running. Meals had to be served. Life had to go on as usual.

Many of the young people, however, did not have enough to do to keep them busy while the ship was at anchor. One day Captain Kristiansen climbed into the launch and went off to the ship chandler's office. The afternoon was hot. People were bored. The blue water all around looked cool and inviting. Someone decided to go swimming. That was like a signal; everyone else followed. One of the men was a very fine diver. He went up on the bridge and did a handstand on the railing, then pushed himself off and came down in a beautiful, graceful dive. Everyone else clapped and clapped. Then someone else tried it. Soon the young people were jumping off the sides of the ship and having a great time.

It was to this merry scene that Captain Kristiansen returned somewhat later. To say he was upset is putting it mildly. Calling the whole ship's company together, he gave them a good dressing down.

'Don't you know there are sharks in that water?' he asked. 'I leave you for a little while and I come back and you're all jumping off the ship. Do you see any other ships around with people jumping off? How do you think I'd feel if you got eaten by a shark and I had to write home to your parents?'

That ended the swimming.

On a Friday afternoon after eight days in port, George returned from his daily excursion in a very different frame of mind. Standing precariously in the swaying launch, he waved his arms excitedly and shouted at the top of his voice, 'Praise God! The money has come in! Enough to pay all our bills!' An American couple, completely unaware that the ship was waiting for money, had sent a cheque for enough money to cover all the expenses.

Awed by such a dramatic evidence of God's power, the *Logos* people gave thanks to God from the depths of their hearts. That same day at midnight the ship set sail for Lagos, Nigeria. As if to add the final evidence of God's blessing, that evening permission was finally obtained to show a Billy Graham film, 'The Restless Ones' with a Spanish sound-track. It was the first time a gospel film had ever been shown to the general public in Las Palmas. It was shown to a packed house in the centre of town.

The ten-day voyage to Lagos went smoothly. For many non-crew members it was a time of relaxation, an opportunity to catch up on letter-writing or to spend time in getting better acquainted with others on board. For the crew, of course, work went on as usual. One job was the setting up of a structure to house the book exhibition. Back in Rotterdam a decision had finally been reached that the book exhibition should be located under a tent on the foredeck. A tentmaker in Holland had come aboard, sized up the situation and returned home to make a tent to cover the area. Now Ebbo Buurma and Albert van der Kuijl had the task of building a construction on which to hang the tent. The job was not as simple as it might sound. To begin with, two huge cranes were located on the foredeck. The tent, which was in two parts, had to fit around these cranes. Another complication was that the two men could not even look at the tent because it was buried under the books in the hold. There were no drawings to give them any idea of the plan to be followed.

Refusing to be daunted by such obstacles, they made their own plan. Cables were stretched from the bridge to the mast. Other cables ran along the sides of the ship, supported by poles, which the two men erected. That was as far as they could go. The tent could not be put up until the ship came into port.

Mealtimes were one of the few occasions when almost all the ship people would be together in one place, so that was the time announcements were generally made. One day Captain Kristiansen mentioned that they would be passing a postal boat in the early hours of the morning, and he gave the estimated time of passing. Anyone who had any letters to be posted, he went on, should put them in such-and-such a place by a certain hour. Several people went off afterwards to take advantage of the opportunity. Not until they finished writing their letters did it occur to then to enquire what kind of postage stamps would be needed. That's when they discovered they had been taken in by the captain's particular brand of humour.

Mike Wiltshire, who was doing the line-up for Lagos, had flown ahead to Nigeria when the ship left Vigo, Spain. This gave him over two weeks to make arrangements for the arrival of the ship. His experience in London and in Vigo had taught him some of the basics in dealing with port matters. As he wrestled with the problem of planning a programme, a Christian man who ran an import-export business in Lagos suggested to him, 'Mike, you need a committee to do this. Let's form a committee.'

Mike, of course, had heard the familiar complaint that committees talk a lot and do little, but he decided that the proposal was probably a good one. Nigerian Christians took up the idea enthusiastically. And they did far more than just talk; they acted and proved to be of immense help. So much help, in fact, that forming a local committee of Christian leaders became standard practice in line-up preparations. Many pastors who had lived for years in the same city worked together for the first time in their lives when they served on these committees.

In Lagos a new element was added to the line-up responsibilities. One of the wives on the ship was expecting a baby. Mike had to investigate the hospital situation and make arrangements for her to go somewhere for the birth of the baby. No one could foresee that this would be wasted effort.

The mother-to-be, Loes de Keijzer, had originally wanted the child to be born on the ship, but the midwife, Ann Rossiter, convinced her that, since this was her first baby, it was safer for the birth to take place in a hospital ashore where there would be facilities available in case of emergency. The voyage to Lagos, however, was a long one, and Ann decided to prepare everything in the ship's hospital just in case the baby came early. Nothing happened until the ship reached Lagos, but when labour started, the birth progressed so quickly that there was no time to transfer Loes from her cabin to the hospital ashore. All went well as Ann, assisted by the ship's doctor, delivered a healthy little girl. She was named Ruth.

The first three days of the two-week stay in Nigeria were spent in setting up the book exhibition. This was such a big job that everyone who was not absolutely needed elsewhere on the ship pitched in to help. The foredeck, where the exhibition was to be located, bore some resemblance to an obstacle course. Not only were there two cranes mounted on the deck, there were also two huge openings leading to holds where goods were stored below. The openings (called hatches) were rectangular holes framed by walls built to extend about eighteen inches above the deck. The hatches were covered by thick planks so heavy that two men were required to remove them. During the voyage three VW vans were stored on the top of each of these hatches.

The procedure for setting up the book exhibition, then, was first to shift the vehicles off the hatches. Normally the vehicles would be lifted ashore, but in Nigeria that was not possible, so they were just set aside on the deck. The planks were then removed from the hatches. Men climbed down a ladder into the hold to get the books. What met their eyes was chaos, utter chaos!

In Rotterdam the crew had been able to load things in an orderly way on the ship, but in Britain, when the books and many other supplies had been taken aboard, they had run into a problem. The loading was not done in London, but a short distance away in the River Medway. Because the *Logos* could not come up to the quayside, loading had to be done from barges. Furthermore, trade unions would not allow the *Logos* crew to do their own loading. Indifferent union stevedores had to do it all. Their procedure was to lift up the boxes of books in a huge net, move the load over the opening to the hold, release one side of the net, and plop! all the boxes would tumble down into the hold on top of whatever was already there.

From this jumbled heap of battered boxes, the *Logos* men extracted whichever ones caught their fancy and loaded them onto a wooden pallet which was swung out by crane onto the deck. There a team of workers went through the boxes, taking out a few books from each one until they had what appeared to be a reasonable selection—all rather hit and miss. The rest of the books were returned in their boxes to the holds below, the hatches were closed, and the vehicles returned to their resting places on top of the hatches. Metal shelves were put into position running the length of the deck and the tent hung in place. A miracle, thought Ebbo and Albert, as they saw that the tent fitted perfectly on their handiwork! Finally the books were put on the shelves and artistically arranged on the hatch covers around the wheels of the six vehicles. The first *Logos* book exhibition had been set up. Everyone beamed with pride.

The obvious drawback to the system was how the stock on the exhibition would be replenished when it ran out.

But, thought the *Logos* workers, why worry about that
problem now? Wait and see if the situation arises.

They discovered it was a situation they would have to
face frequently. A procedure was worked out. One of the
hatch covers would be partially exposed so that a couple
of the planks could be removed. This was done at night
after the book exhibition was closed to the public. Someone would climb down the steep ladder into the hold and
begin the search for books. All this had to be done in total
darkness except for the light of the big torch he carried. A
human chain would be formed up the ladder. As the man
with the torch located some books, he would pass them to
the man at the bottom of the ladder who would hand them
up to the next man and so on. It was a long, laborious
process, made all the more difficult by the completely
haphazard way the books had been stored below.

The *Logos* leaders had not really thought about the
problem of restocking the book exhibition shelves,
because they really didn't expect to have to restock them.
The ship was going to be in Lagos for only two weeks.
After all, how often does a normal bookshop need to
replenish the books on display?

To the amazement of everyone on the *Logos*, hundreds
of people came to visit the ship every day. Curiosity drew
them. The novelty of being on a ship was intriguing. As
they wandered around the book exhibition, various books
caught their attention and they bought them. Cookery
books, big colourful children's books, dictionaries,
Bibles, and one of the most popular, *How to Have a
Happy Marriage*. For the first time workers on the *Logos*
began to realise that the ship itself could be an attraction,
that large numbers of people who would shrug aside the
invitation to an event on land would flock to the same
event on board a ship.

The exhibition was mostly educational books with only
a few Christian ones. However, at the Christian leaders'
conference on board, a display of Christian books was set

up. A large number of Christian books had been donated to the ship by various publishers. These could therefore be sold much more cheaply than usual. Some of the Nigerian Christians left the ship carrying boxes of Christian books.

On Sundays the ship closed down and the people went ashore for meetings. Only a handful of men remained on the ship to keep watch. The rest of the crew and staff were put on teams going to different churches to sing, to describe the ways God had worked in their own lives or to give a message from God's word. On the first Sunday the *Logos* was in Nigeria, seventeen such meetings were scheduled. After the church services the people from the *Logos* were invited to the homes of some of the very warm-hearted and hospitable Nigerians and were given an opportunity to sample Nigerian cooking and to get to know Nigerian families.

During the two weeks in Lagos, what was to become the usual programme was carried out. Evangelistic teams passed out tracts, went door-to-door with Christian books and held open-air meetings. Other meetings took place in churches, schools or wherever there was opportunity. A Christian leaders' conference was held, and tours of the ship were given.

The doctors who had sailed with the ship to the Canary Islands and to Lagos had come on a temporary basis only, because the long-term doctor was not able to come in time for the first voyages. In Lagos the new doctor arrived; Dr Norman MacPherson, an older Scottish retired missionary who had worked as a doctor in India. When he came on board, the chief steward, who was in charge of assigning cabins, decided he should be put in the cabin that was being occupied by Peter Conlan. Peter would have to move into another cabin with someone else. The only problem was that Peter had gone ashore on business and might not return for several hours. After some deliberation, the chief steward decided that the doctor should be settled immediately. Peter's belongings were taken from his cupboard and drawers, packed into boxes and deposited in his new quarters. When he returned about three hours later, he went to his old cabin, opened the door and was shocked to see a strange man lying in his bed. All trace of his occupancy had been removed. Peter's reaction could hardly be described as 'spiritual'. He has since often quoted the old lines:

'To live above with saints we love,
Oh t'will be such glory;
But to live below with saints we know
Is quite a different story.'

These were the kinds of incidents that kept the *Logos* people aware of their need of God. Without his presence and work in their lives, the ship could easily become a floating hotbed of tensions and in-fighting and any hope of ministry for God would be gone. Each individual had to learn to go to God and to one another and ask forgiveness for careless, inconsiderate acts, for flare-ups of temper, for hasty judgements, for all kinds of action that could damage personal relationships.

The voyage to South Africa was a beautiful one. On board people were relaxed and happy, looking forward to their next new experience. When the ship arrived in Capetown, South Africa, her leaders made their position very clear. There could be no segregation aboard the ship. The authorities agreed to this. However, workers on the *Logos* noticed with interest that during the day, so-called coloureds and blacks came to the book exhibition, but hardly any whites. In the evening all the whites came, only whites. But business was slow. Many times there would be no more than twenty people browsing around in the book exhibition.

That went on for several days. Then came the first Sunday. Philip Morris, who was now the book exhibition manager, was returning with a team from a church service ashore. Coming into the port area they saw a long line of several hundred people. Who were all these people? they wondered. What was the show? Where were they going? Slowly the realisation dawned. These people were lining up to get on *Logos*! How unbelievable! What was happening was that people on their way home from church were stopping to visit the ship. On that day the book exhibitions recorded more than £600 in sales.

At the end of the visit to Capetown, George Verwer announced elatedly to the ship company, 'For the first time we've been able to pay all our bills with the money from book sales.'

The next port of call, a very brief call, was at Mombasa, Kenya. The two line-up men who had gone ahead ran into a problem there. No berth was available for the ship. As the time of the ship's arrival drew near, panic began to set in. Again they were made aware of their dependence on God. Surely he had a solution. As they prayed and continued looking for a possible answer, a large cement company made available a berth that was normally used exclusively for company business. The berth was in an excellent location not far from the centre of town.

Even though the time in Mombasa was short, a conference was held for Christian leaders. One hundred attended, some of them coming from as far as four hundred miles away. About half of them actually lived on the ship. Single ship men and women on the *Logos* freely gave up their cabins and slept in the lounge or out on deck in order to give their African brothers a comfortable place to stay.

For the first time the closed-circuit television system which had been installed in Rotterdam was used. Because the dining-room was the largest room on the ship, the conference was held there. The messages were given in English, but people who preferred to hear them in Swahili were seated in a smaller room nearby. There they could watch the speaker on the television monitor but hear the simultaneous translation in Swahili.

The entire company of the ship, crew and staff, could hardly wait to get to India. This was the final goal! This was what the ship was all about; bringing literature, vehicles, supplies and people to India so teams could move out and work there! During the last leg of the voyage to India, there was even an argument about the speed of the ship. George couldn't wait; he wanted the ship to move full speed ahead. As the morning of 12 May began to dawn, the shores of Cochin, India could just dimly be distinguished. Unable to contain himself any longer, George called the ship's company together on the bow of the ship to have a time of prayer, rejoicing and praise to God.

As the ship moved into the narrow channel leading to Cochin, Indian OMers crowded into a rented launch and set out to meet the *Logos*. The Indians, many of them known to people on board, stood in the launch, waving their Bibles over their heads and shouting Bible verses at the top of their lungs. Interspersed with the verses were shouts of joy and praise to God. The ship, *God's* ship, had reached Cochin!

No sooner had the ship docked in what appeared to be a little fishing town than George Verwer leaped down the gangway, flew across the wooden pier and knelt down to kiss the soil of India. For three or four years he had worked in India and loved it. Then, because of a complicated situation with immigration officials, he was blacklisted. As part of the *Logos* crew and staff, however, he was able to enter the country that was otherwise forbidden to him. Seven years later he described his feelings of that moment to a group of new recruits for the *Logos*:

'I cannot tell you what an experience that was! I was a man without permission to go into India. I could no longer get a visa and had not seen India for a couple of years. Yet here I was on the *Logos* sailing into Cochin! I'm almost crying now to talk about it. I just wept with joy to be back in India, something I had prayed for since 1968.'

Others on the ship might not have been so exuberant in their expressions of joy and exultation, but they too felt it deeply. As Ebbo Buurma put it, 'We felt just like Columbus must have felt when he set foot in America. The greatest thing on earth was for us to be in Cochin!'

7

The miracle ship?

To the men and women lining the rails of the *Logos* as she sailed into port, Cochin appeared to be a small fishing village. That impression was misleading. The port area, its banks strewn with fishing nets, turned out to be a good distance from the centre of Cochin and its larger neighbour, the city of Ernakulam. To complicate matters, a local bus strike eliminated public transport to the port area. In spite of this difficulty, crowds of people streamed toward the ship, many of them walking miles in order to get there. For the ship workers, it was a busy time, giving tours, selling books, holding meetings, showing films, and distributing tracts.

In Cochin a new first engineer arrived with his family. A highly-qualified man, he was greatly needed, but his arrival was nevertheless viewed with some trepidation. All we need, thought the crew, is a loudmouthed, inconsiderate American—a Texan, at that—throwing his weight around.

Mike Poynor's appearance on the scene blasted all their stereotyped preconceptions to smithereens. A tall, solidly-built man, Mike turned out to be a calm, stable person; quiet, unassuming yet brilliant. As one of the crew later put it, 'Mike had that rare ability to enforce respect in a mature way.' He was to become a valuable asset to the ship ministry throughout the coming years.

Mike's wife, Carol Ann, describes coming to the ship with their two small daughters:

'We flew into Bombay and went the rest of the way by train. When the train pulled into the station in Bombay, it was so packed we put our kids through the window; Mike climbed through the window; he grabbed me through the window and George Miley shoved our suitcases through the window. We were on the train for two days and two nights, third class, unreserved. When you moved your foot, someone sat there. If you moved your elbow, someone sat there. But the Indian people were fantastic! They fed us—the kids got sick; we got sick—but the people were so loving, so kind. It was just an unbelievable orientation to India. I have had a very deep love for India ever since.

'When we arrived in Cochin, my husband went straight to the engine room—I think he may have changed his clothes in the process. I unpacked and settled into the cabin somewhat.

'Two days later the ship pulled out of Cochin. The next three weeks I don't remember at all. Someone else took care of my children and I just flaked out, seasick. It was only after eight years on the ships that I finally got to the point where I could actually do something at sea. I learned how to clean a hallway at sea and things like that, though I got sick several times while doing it.

'I had a fear of living with so many Christian women in such close quarters. When we joined the ship, there was one washing machine, just one washing machine on the entire ship. You got to use it, if you had children, twice a week; if you didn't have children, once a week. Yet there was never an argument. That to me was so exciting. It just showed that the Lord was in this place.'

On the day before the *Logos* was to leave Cochin, one of the crew was working on some refrigeration machinery on the foredeck when a ministry leader came by and said someone was needed to speak in a meeting ashore that evening. Could he do it? He accepted with alacrity. After all, that was why he was here—to minister to people.

Leaving his tools and machinery standing on the deck, he rushed off to change clothes and prepare hurriedly for the meeting.

Next morning his boss let him know in no uncertain terms what he thought of such behaviour. How did he dare drop his work and go off without a word to his boss? And whatever possessed him to leave all his working gear strewn about the deck? Stung by the rebuke, the luckless crew member defended himself heatedly, matching the voice of his superior in volume and ardour. The two parted angrily.

As the ship pulled away from the pier later that day, the steering gear failed suddenly. Immediately the anchor was dropped. The engine astern did not respond to frantic attempts to start it. The ship was forcefully swung around by the strong current and just barely missed going aground.

The crewman who had been so vociferously rebuked by his boss was horrified by this turn of events. He was reminded of how much the ship depended on God's mercy. Overwhelmed with the realisation of just how wrongly he had behaved, he confessed it all to God. Then, humbling himself, he went to his superior to ask for forgiveness.

Whatever bearing the crewman's situation may have had on the rest of the ship, the technical difficulties were sorted out and the ship proceeded with all her vital equipment in running order.

After a short visit to the small city of Tuticorin, the *Logos* sailed into Madras, totally unprepared for what would take place there. One of the public relations men, thinking back over all God had done in making the ship project a reality, had prepared a small publicity brochure entitled *The miracle ship*. Picked up by the media, the title captured the attention of the Indian people. Thousands of them flocked to the ship, expecting to see dramatic healings and other kinds of miracles. Long lines of people would stand for hours in the hot sun, waiting patiently for their chance to board the ship. Of course, to accommodate such a vast number of visitors, those who boarded had to be whisked through the ship as fast as possible. Some of the *Logos* women, standing idly at the rail, noticed a woman with a conspicuous red dress coming aboard. They decided to time her visit. Exactly six minutes after she set foot on the deck, she was on the gangway descending from the ship. Describing the scene, Ebbo Buurma said:

> 'The miracle was that we survived at all! I remember one day we counted up to 15,000 people coming to the *Logos*. I'm sure some people never even touched the decks of the *Logos* because they were just hanging between the man in front of them and the man behind them. They were simply squeezed over the ship and couldn't see anything. The book exhibition turned into a total disaster. At one time the bookshelves were turned over because people were so squeezed together.
>
> 'We survived it after all, and everybody who left the ship got at least a tract. Total sales on that particular day with 15,000 people were more or less 900 rupees, which was probably equivalent to something like £45. Anyway, I think that was the first time we really saw that the ship could be made very attractive, but we also saw it could be very dangerous to get so many people in one go. However, it was all very exciting to see the enormous interest which, of course, we had to learn to control a little bit better.'

Better control of the crowds was necessary, not just to make the visits to the ship more enjoyable, but also to make them safer. In Madras the ship was continually moving up and down in the water, so the foot of the gangway rested on rollers. As the ship bobbed up and down, the bottom of the gangway would roll back and forth a bit. When the crowds pressed forward to swarm onto the ship, the people in front could easily get a foot caught under the moving gangway. All the mental and physical resources of the *Logos* people were needed to devise ways to hold back the people so they could mount the gangway in an orderly manner. One *Logos* worker took a lady's arm to help her on board. Her Muslim husband, misinterpreting the gesture, stormed toward him with murder in his eyes. Undoubtedly setting a track record, the *Logos* man leaped up the gangway and took refuge in one of the bathrooms, locking himself securely in. George Verwer came to the rescue and attempted to explain that the man from the *Logos* was only trying to help. Eventually, after being given a private tour of the engine room, the offended husband calmed down and the crisis passed.

After this, the *Logos* company began to wonder if the publicity materials should be re-evaluated and the term 'Miracle Ship' dropped. They also hit on an effective way of weeding out the curiosity seekers from the serious buyers among the visitors to the book exhibition. An entrance fee of twenty-five paise (about 1 p) was charged. This could be put towards any purchase in the book exhibition. In spite of this restriction, about 100,000 people passed through the ship during the six-week visit to Madras. Every one of them went away with at least a tract explaining the message of the Saviour and his love for them. The fastest-moving item on the book exhibition was a 'Gospel packet', which contained two Gospels, two Christian booklets and a letter from the captain giving the background of the ship. Thousands of these packets were sold.

Perhaps the most significant contribution of the ship to the local churches came through the volunteer programme. About fifty Indian young people became involved in this, working as volunteers in every part of the ship from the pantry to the engine room or the book exhibition. Not only did they work side by side with the *Logos* men and women in practical jobs, they also accompanied them on various forms of evangelism. For many of these young people this was the first time they had ever actively been involved in telling other people about Jesus Christ.

As the visit to Madras drew to an end, the time of the yearly monsoons approached. What should the *Logos* do during these weeks? Simply lie up somewhere and wait for the storms to pass, or move to some quieter place? Captain Kristiansen, with his experience in Indonesia and his great love for the people there, was quite vocal in letting his opinion be known. He was virtually the only one on the ship who knew anything about Indonesia, but the ship leaders decided that the idea of a visit to that country might be worth a try.

Sailing with the ship to Indonesia (with a stop on the way in Singapore) were a number of Indians. Many of the original ship's company had disembarked in India to work there. Their places were taken by Indians or by Western OMers whose visas for India had expired. There were several Indian crew members as well as a group of potential Indian leaders who had come for training.

Having absolutely no idea of what to expect in Indonesia, the *Logos* company was amazed at the openness of the people. Perhaps this, more than anything else, made the OMers aware of the potential for the ship's ministry outside India. More than 8,000 people attended rallies in the indoor sports stadium where George Verwer preached his heart out. As many as 500 people at a time would watch films with an Indonesian sound-track shown on the side of the ship each evening. From not only Surabaja but all over Java requests came in for teams to take meetings; more requests than the ship could handle. Every night the ship vans, off-loaded on the shore, would stand ready to transport people from the ship to various parts of the city to pass out tracts, which were eagerly received.

Many Indonesians came to the ship and offered their services as volunteer workers in various parts of the ship. The deck department alone had ten local men working alongside them in the necessary but boring job of chipping off rust. Many of these volunteers were deeply influenced by their close contact with the ship personnel and by the teaching they were given on the ship. Several realised they were not even Christians and decided to commit their lives to Jesus Christ.

Everywhere they went, the *Logos* workers saw people respond to the message of new life in Christ.

With such wide-open doors it was hard for the *Logos* to leave Indonesia, but it was time to return to Singapore for dry dock. The ship by this time was so laden with growth on the bottom of her hull that her speed was significantly reduced. In dry dock that was all cleaned off and various repairs and overhauling of machinery was also done.

Many of the people on the ship had sailed from Europe with the idea of working one year. Now they needed to return home and be replaced by new recruits. The original idea of the ship commuting between India and Britain had to be shelved when the Suez Canal closed in 1967. If the ship couldn't go all the way to Europe without the long trip around Africa, at least she should go as close as possible to make things easier for the change-over of personnel. The closest place was Kuwait in the Gulf (called the Arabian Gulf by the Arabs and the Persian Gulf by the Iranians. The *Logos* once found herself in a predicament when one of her crew inadvertently referred to it by the wrong name to the wrong person.)

As the ship was going to be in the Gulf anyway, it was decided that she should visit some of the other countries as well, to get a feel of the situation there. Since the Gulf was such a stronghold of Islam, ship people didn't anticipate being able to do any kind of evangelism, but perhaps they could somehow serve as an encouragement and stimulus to the few struggling churches of Indians and other expatriates. At any rate, just the fact that a Christian ship could enter this part of the world would be a testimony of God's power.

The first port of call in the Gulf was Dubai. *Logos* was the only ship in port. There was only one berth and it wasn't completely finished. A tour of the city at that time took only fifteen minutes. The visit of the ship was a big event for the people there. Everyone went to see it. Being a very sociable people they seemed to enjoy just standing around and chatting. Impressive and somewhat intimidating they were, in their long flowing robes with long vicious-looking knives strapped to their waists. To ship people who were unaccustomed to such sights, they were like a scene from *Arabian Nights*. Their Mercedes-Benz cars, however, were thoroughly modern. So was their hunger for books. Having no budgeting restraints, they bought freely: sets of encyclopedias; expensive books of full-colour photographs; whatever caught their fancy.

Philip Morris tells a story which has become part of *Logos* folklore:

'In Dubai an extremely rich man came to the ship in his Rolls-Royce. He came on board to buy books and he'd just got a new wife (he already had two) who was Lebanese, an air hostess. He walked around the book exhibition, saying, "Oh, I'll have that and that and that," pointing to all the big books, including a set of Encyclopaedia Britannica. He made sure the latter was a different colour from the two he already had. "I've only got one in blue and one in green," he explained, "so I want one in red."

'He had collected quite a pile of books, to our delight, when his wife came up to him and enquired in an affected British accent, "Darling, is that all you've got?"

' "Oh no," he hastily replied, "I'm having this, this, this, this . . ." and pointed suddenly to a few dozen other books.

'Zoom! We got those books at record speed and piled them up.

'"OK," he said, "you make the bill out. I'll send my driver to collect everything tomorrow."

'The next day the driver came in a Jaguar, paid the bill and carried off the books.

'Now, when we had been in Denmark, where we bought the ship, the Faroese Seaman's Mission had given us a tooth from a narwhal. That's a whale that has a tooth that develops into a sort of spiral-shaped horn similar to what a unicorn is imagined to have. This one stood about four feet high.

'Our wealthy visitor heard about the whale's tooth from the teacher of one of his children and he wanted it. This was something that no one else in the Gulf had because it was common only in the area around Denmark. So he sent some-one to tell us that he wanted it.

'We had a little meeting to consider the matter. Should we sell it to him? We decided we would. We were sure the Faroese people would be happy for the money to go to God's work. But what price? Finally the decision was left to me.

'"Well, I'm going to ask for 500 dinars (about £600)."

'They all thought I was crazy, but if I wanted to do it, that was OK with them.

'The following day the man came to me and said abruptly, "I want the whale's tooth." Just like that.

' "But we haven't discussed the price," I objected.

'"It's irrelevant."

'Turning to his driver, he ordered, "Put it in the car." And back to me, "How much do you want?"

' "I want 500 dinars."

'Casually he put his hand in his pocket, pulled out some bills, handed me 500 dinars and walked off.'

The change-over of personnel was accomplished, four ports in the Gulf were visited and the ship returned to India. Shortly before the year's end, the ship said good-bye to Captain Kristiansen for a few months. He was taking a leave of absence for a very important reason; to get married to Ann Rossiter, the young English midwife he had come to know on the *Logos*. Conducting a court-ship in the small, tight-knit community of the *Logos* must not have been easy. Everything the couple did was watched with affectionate amusement or vicarious delight. But they made it safely through the often frustrat-ing circumstances and were married in Oslo, Norway on 16 December. A retired British officer, Captain George Paget, stood in for Kristiansen during his absence from the *Logos*.

1971 was also remarkable for the birth of the Intensive Training (IT) programme. During the OM summer cam-paigns in Europe, George Verwer had become very enthusiastic about the Outward Bound courses that were becoming popular in Britain and America at that time.

The idea of the courses was to put young people into situations (usually involving challenging outdoor sports) where they were stretched to the limit, and discovered resources within themselves they never knew they had. A great feature of these challenges was that they took place in small teams where the young people could learn a lot about themselves and their relationships with others.

Typically, George adapted and modified this concept to include spiritual as well as physical challenges. Typically, too, the goals he set were slightly 'over the top' for this first year. For a start, the programme was to take place not for one or two weeks, but over six long months. Then, the goals set included so many tracts to be distributed, hours of work to be done, books to be sold, Christian films to be watched and tapes to be listened to, Bible passages to be read, Bible studies to be carried out, letters to be written, long literature-distribution treks to be undertaken (carrying no provisions, in faith that God would supply all needs), as well as the physical goals for running and exercises, that the young men who had been 'volunteered' for the programme reckoned they would need a 16-hour day just to meet the goals, without time for eating, resting, or the other essentials of life.

The small group of young men, many of whom had only just joined the ship, were not enthusiastic. And they did not become more enthusiastic as they ploughed through their goals. They certainly found out more about themselves—one of them, Jud Lamos, said later:

> 'One thing the IT programme did was to turn us into the most carnal, the most self-seeking people imaginable. Everything the Bible says not to do, we did, just to get those goals done . . .'

In fact, not one of the young men succeeded in reaching all those goals. It was impossible to do. Yet the surprising thing is that every one who went through that first IT programme looks back on it as an extremely profitable experience that contributed immensely to his personal and spiritual development. Jud Lamos analysed it like this:

'We were faced with problems that we tried to overcome as a team, working individually or with each other, saying, "Here's our goal. This is what we're going to do." Sometimes most of us would be down, but someone who was up would encourage us to go forward. We learned principles that could be applied successfully in the business world as well; realising how much more you can get out of a person who is already stretched, but also realising when you need to go and work with that person and support him rather than trying to get him to work for you. A lot of that came out in IT.

'In terms of spiritual warfare, the benefits were even greater. We all had to come to the place where we saw that we were trying to do everything in our own strength. We were busy all the time trying to meet our goals and in this busy-ness we were getting so far away from the Lord. We needed to go to the Lord and confess that in spite of all our lofty goals, we were just a black pit inside.

'I remember sitting in the ship's library one night about two months before the end of my IT time. I went through a whole list of questions about what I was doing, and in the end there was only one thing I was still sure of—the existence of God. I felt stripped of every belief that I had. I remember realising how much I needed Jesus to cleanse me and pleading with him to do so . . . then the Lord broke through to me in a marvellous way and changed my heart so that I wasn't concerned about goals any more. I still wanted to meet the goals, but they weren't the overriding purpose in my life.'

The IT programme, which had begun with reluctance on the part of the participants, had produced such positive results that it became a standard feature of the ship. One of the ministry leaders, Frank Dietz, was given the responsibility for it. He, in turn, refined and developed it. Being accepted to participate in the IT programme became a privilege. A number of people who would serve as leaders in various OM fields as well as with other missions received some of their most significant personal and leadership development experiences in the Intensive Training programme.

8

Healing the wounds

On a December evening in 1971 the *Logos* sailed into
Bombay, a city teeming with humanity. It lay in complete
darkness. Not a light was to be seen anywhere. The *Logos*
was escorted in by a submarine. Men came aboard and
sealed off her radio. War had just been declared between
India and Pakistan over what was then called East
Pakistan.

The *Logos* company soon discovered that in spite of the
occasional sound of gunfire or the sight of a tracer rocket
lighting up the sky, there was no physical danger. The
gunfire was only a stage effect to make the people aware
of the war that was going on far away. Nevertheless the
Logos was somewhat hampered in her programme and
decided to move farther south to Goa and come back later
to Bombay.

While the ship was in Goa, the war came to an end. The
whole Indian fleet, led by the Admiral of the Navy, filed
into Goa to celebrate the victory. Someone on the *Logos*
got the idea of inviting the officers from these ships for a
Christmas banquet as a means of outreach to them. Elaborate gilt-edged invitations were printed. Formal dress
was indicated. When the time came, the Indian officers
appeared, splendid in their dress uniforms. The only

uniforms the *Logos* officers had, however, were casual short-sleeved cotton ones. In spite of this social awkwardness the evening went well and the Indian officers seemed to enjoy themselves. As one of the *Logos* officers' wife commented years later, 'I think we were all so young we got away with a lot of things we couldn't do now. We had food so tough they couldn't even cut it. I remember when they cut the traditional British Christmas pudding, it was so hard it bounced out of the bowls.'

The *Logos* people were to have a much closer look at the effects of the war, for on 19 April the *Logos* sailed into the newly-created country of Bangladesh. The fighting had ended, though an occasional shot could still be heard. The ravages of war were to be seen everywhere. Sunken wrecks littered the harbour areas. Blown-up bridges hampered travel. People with gunshots and all kinds of minor injuries gathered in little boats around the foot of the *Logos* gangway to receive medical attention from the ship's nurses.

The *Logos* first went up river to the small city of Chalna. There she had to stay at anchor, as did all the other ships in the port. Not long after her arrival a violent storm broke suddenly on the area, with winds so strong they ripped to shreds the canvas coverings from the lifeboats and from the top of the poop deck. Some of the *Logos* crew, out on deck to observe the storm, were startled to see the upright body of a man come sweeping down the middle of the river at tremendous speed. In his hands he clutched an oar, which he waved frantically as he screamed for help. The *Logos* onlookers realised that he must be sitting in a small boat submerged beneath the water.

'We've got to rescue him!' was the instinctive reaction of the *Logos* crew.

'Absolutely not! There's nothing we can do,' said the captain. 'To try to lower a rescue boat in this storm would be suicide.'

The man at sea had hardly passed the *Logos* when the storm died down just as quickly as it had started. Several of the crew, at the quick command of the captain, rushed to lower a motor boat and take off after the man. Catching up with the swamped boat, they pulled the man into the safety of their own boat. Rather than collapsing from relief at his spectacular rescue, he began talking hysterically and gesturing frantically toward his little boat, obviously terrified that it might be left to perish. Obligingly, his rescuers tied it to their motor boat and towed it back to the ship.

When they pulled up alongside the ship, one of the crew lifted the dripping wet, trembling, thoroughly frightened Bengali man and carried him aboard. Before the poor man had time to collect his wits, Susanne Lindeman, a proper German nurse, whisked him off to the shower and subjected him to what was probably the most thorough washing he had ever had in his life. Then he was stuffed full of medicine and tucked into bed in the ship's hospital to rest and recover from his shock.

In the meantime, some of the crew pumped the water out of his boat. A day or so later he was taken back to his village. To the astonishment of the crew members with him, the villagers began to shower them with a barrage of questions, not about the man's health and safety, but about the boat. To these people the boat represented life. It was their means of earning money to live.

The Ship's doctor, Dr Arrawattigi, an elderly Indian man, was deeply disturbed when he heard there were a couple of million people in the outlying villages without the services of a single doctor. With two of the ship's nurses he would climb each morning into one of the ship's motorised lifeboats and head up-river to some of the villages where he would hold a clinic in the market-place. All day long the medical team would work, coming back late in the evening. Often they would be accompanied by other *Logos* workers as well, who would ask a local Christian to translate while they talked about Jesus Christ to groups of villagers gathered in the central square of the village. People listened with great interest.

One morning Dr Arrawattigi spoke in morning devotions on the ship. As he reviewed his life, he said, 'I can say with the Apostle Paul, "I have fought a good fight. I have finished the course." '

Two or three mornings later, one of his Indian helpers went to the doctor's cabin to wake him up. When there was no response to the knock, he opened the door and stepped inside the cabin to investigate. He saw Dr Arrawattigi lying peacefully on the bed. A closer look revealed that only the body lay there; the spirit had gone home to God. Sometime during the night the doctor had died of a heart attack.

When Dr Arrawattigi's son and son-in-law came to take the body back to India, Ebbo Buurma told them how their father had saved his son's life:.

'André had been born on the ship when it was in Bombay, and he was only a few months old. His brother Stefan had been given some sweets while we were in India. Stefan took one of the pieces and sucked the chocolate off. Then when Vera and I weren't looking, he took the peanut which was inside and stuffed it into the baby's mouth.

'All of a sudden Vera and I saw that André wasn't breathing any more because the peanut had gone into his windpipe. Vera grabbed him and slapped him on the back, but the peanut wouldn't come out. She shot out of the cabin like lightning and went to Susanne Lindeman's cabin. Both nurses were there. They struggled like mad to get the kid breathing again, but he wouldn't start breathing. He turned purple instead.

'All of a sudden, as if by a miracle, Dr Arrawattigi happened to pass by the hospital and saw what was going on. Without stopping to think, he just opened the little mouth of the baby—he was a huge man with big fingers—and he stuffed his finger with full force into the throat of the baby and pulled out that peanut. With a noisy rattling sound, the baby gasped and began to breathe again. Turning to me, the doctor said, "Brother, your son has been born again today."

He would certainly have died if Dr Arrawattigi had not rescued him.'

The lofty, idealistic plans to use *Logos* for relief work
were brought down to reality with a bang when she
arrived in the first country that really needed relief supplies. In Calcutta there were huge warehouses full of
supplies that various organisations had donated for
Bangladesh. The bottleneck was distribution. Negotiations were undertaken for *Logos* to spend a couple of
months shuttling back and forth between Calcutta and
Bangladesh to deliver these supplies. But the Bangladesh
customs authorities raised so many difficulties that the
idea had to be abandoned.

The holds of the *Logos* were full of used clothing that
had been donated for Bangladesh. For this, customs presented no difficulty. The problem came from other quarters. Missionaries were asked if they could take the
clothing to distribute, but no one wanted it. There was so
much rivalry that unless there were twenty-six blue
T-shirts exactly alike, they wouldn't take them; it would
cause too much squabbling. The Red Cross didn't want
the clothing either. Finally, the Red Cross agreed to send
a truck to the ship as it lay by the quayside in Chittagong
and load the vehicle with used clothing. The truck took it
to the market-place and simply dumped it there. It disappeared like magic. At least it got into the hands of people
who needed it.

With this injection of realism, the plans for relief work
began to fade away, pushed out by new horizons of ministry that were opening up for the ship.

In Chittagong a Bengali came aboard and asked to
meet someone from the crew. He began talking with one
of the engineers, explaining his great desire to see Christian professionals come to Bangladesh to work. Muslims,
he explained, tended to look on missionaries as paid
workers, talking about religion because that was their job.
But if people in secular jobs talked about Christ they

would have a much wider range of contacts and much more scope to talk freely to people who would listen more readily and openmindedly.

The *Logos* engineer listened with keen interest. A few years later he did return to Bangladesh to work in a secular job. He taught engineering and was able to talk about Jesus Christ from the perspective of a professional in the shipping world.

During the time in Bangladesh a group from the *Logos* went to the capital city of Dhaka, going overland by truck. A few journeyed by paddleboat up-river from the *Logos* to transport books to an exhibition that would be set up in a hall of the university in Dhaka.

The university itself was a sad place to see. Its buildings were pockmarked by bullets. Within its walls many of the intelligentsia of the country had been killed. Long strands of human hair lay strewn about in trees and bushes, grim reminders of the three or four hundred university women who had been herded into a compound to be used as prostitutes. In desperation many had hanged themselves by their long hair, so all the hair had been cut off and thrown out.

It was to this university campus that a *Logos* team came with books. A large number of these educational books were donated to help restock the university library, which had suffered great destruction. A book exhibition was set up in one of the university halls. Books were offered for sale at greatly reduced prices.

The hall where the exhibition was held was on the ground floor with many doors opening out to a grassy area outside. After two or three days the exhibition workers became aware of the fact that a lot of stealing was taking place. They responded by closing all the doors except one and barricading them with stacks of chairs. Gradually becoming wise to the situation, they were able to spot various faces that kept reappearing in the exhibition. The thieves would separate as they entered the exhibition and each go his own way, unobtrusively collecting whatever books he wanted, giving the impression that when he was finished he would proceed to the cash desk to pay for his selection. At a given signal the gang would suddenly all charge toward a certain one of the closed doors. Confederates outside the hall would have removed the barricade of chairs, thus freeing the way of the thieves inside to fling open the doors and disappear into the open spaces beyond.

Book exhibition workers responded to this new development by posting people outside to check the doors periodically. That effectively put an end to the most blatant of the stealing.

Every day the band of thieves would come and roam the book exhibition, looking for some possibility to open up for them. Book exhibition workers, recognising them, would often go up to some of them and start a conversation, thinking that as long as they were talking they couldn't be getting into mischief. Every day the frustration of the thieves increased, until the final day when the tension neared the point of explosion. They were desperate to find some last opportunity to get books. When the time came to close the exhibition, they wouldn't leave. Book exhibition workers stood around uneasily, not knowing how to handle the situation. One of them finally went out to get a policeman to come and clear out the problem-makers. With the entrance of the police, the atmosphere crackled with tension as each side sized up the other. In the end, it was the thieves who backed down and left quietly.

In July, after visits to three other countries on the way, the *Logos* arrived in the Philippines. The country at that time was facing many problems. A typhoon bringing eighteen inches of rain had struck the Manila area just the day before the ship arrived. A ship beached up on the shore gave mute testimony to the ferocity of the storm.

The physical destruction was only a very small part of the problems confronting the Philippines, as the ship's company soon discovered. To prevent books from being stolen, the *Logos* leaders decided a search was necessary as people left the exhibition. One of the book exhibition workers noticed a large man with a suspicious-looking bulge under his shirt. With all the zeal of a crusader about to expose evil, he went up to the man and jerked up his shirt. There lay a gun.

'Uh . . . sorry,' stammered the *Logos* man as he hastily backed away. Thereafter he would temper his zeal with a bit more discretion.

By this time the *Logos* had developed the practice of holding a reception to mark the opening of the book exhibition in a port. They would try to get the highest-ranking official available to be guest of honour. In the Philippines, as usual, the line-up man started at the top in his search for a guest of honour. To his surprise, the president of the Philippines accepted the invitation.

Several hours before the arrival of President Marcos security guards came aboard and carried out an exhaustive search of the ship. Protocol people came to explain just how everything should be done. Closer to the time of the president's arrival a huge company of at least two hundred bodyguards came aboard, well outnumbering the *Logos* crew and staff. They took up positions all over the ship, in every alleyway, in the engine room, in the galley. Every single person on the *Logos* was watched. Two helicopters hovered overhead. Frogmen dived under the ship to check for limpet mines. A couple of speed boats stood by in case of emergency.

When all this was completed, the president came aboard with his wife and his daughter, who was about twelve years old. He was received with ceremony and presented with a couple of gifts from the exhibition; a beautiful, numbered, first-edition copy of the *Living Bible* and a big full colour book about horses, a special interest of his. His wife was presented with an art book, and his daughter with a beautiful children's book.

The president proceeded to address the ship's company in a speech that was recorded to be beamed out on nationwide television and radio that evening. He began by welcoming the ship to the Philippines and went on to say, 'There are seven thousand islands in the Philippines . . . '

'Daddy,' a small voice interrupted, 'there are seven thousand and one hundred.'

Laughter echoed through the room. Stiffness disappeared and the people relaxed to listen to the remainder of the speech.

The president had a few nice words to say about the ship, including a statement that would be quoted many times in years to come: 'This ship is like a mini-United Nations. But there is one difference. You are all united.'

A couple of days after the president's visit to the ship an invitation came from him. The entire ship's company was invited to the palace for a meal—an invitation that was readily accepted by everyone not required to stay on the ship to keep watch. The guests were entertained by a troupe of folk dancers presenting some of the most typical and picturesque of the Philippine dances. Afterwards gifts were presented to everyone. A list of the ship leaders and officers had been requested beforehand. Each was listed by his official title: ship director; ship captain; chief officer; first, second and third officers; chief engineer; first, second and third engineers. With great ceremony a large beautifully-wrapped box was presented to George Miley who was director at that time. An equally large box was presented to the captain. A somewhat smaller box was presented to the chief officer. The first officer received a still smaller box, and so on for the second and third officers. No boxes for the engineers. Apparently whoever was in charge had not realised that they were also officers. They received a small medallion engraved with a picture of the president and his wife, the same medallion which was presented to all the rest of the ship's company. An inadvertent slight, that was to stir up a hornet's nest among the ship's officers.

The visit of the president to the ship opened doors for the *Logos* everywhere and the publicity generated by the visit and the televised speech brought masses of people to the book exhibition. The ship's singing group was asked to participate in a top television programme one Friday evening. Along with the music they were able to explain something of what Christ had done in their own lives.

Many of the *Logos* people participated in church meetings on shore. The pastors' conference on board the ship had to be cancelled before it was finished, unfortunately. A storm blew up. Even though the ship was tied up to the quayside, it bounced and rolled so much that one by one the pastors began to disappear from the meeting and take refuge in the beds in their cabins, where they were miserably seasick.

Not only the pastors' conference was affected by stormy weather. So was the book exhibition. When strong wind and typhoon warnings came, the exhibition had to be moved from the foredeck. An excellent place was found for the exhibition in a big hotel just outside the harbour gates. Sales were better than ever.

'It is so hard to understand that people really needed these books,' said Carol Ann Poynor, who was now working part-time on the book exhibition. 'I remember a nun coming on in the Philippines and she bought some old chemistry textbooks from the United States. They were about twenty years old. I think we gave them to her for about 2p each. She started crying. She just stood there crying because she had been teaching chemistry without a textbook.'

The *Logos* people who were perhaps most deeply affected by the visit of the president to the ship were not even aboard when the ship went to the Philippines in 1972. Gary and Susan Dean joined the ship a few months later. But the second time the *Logos* sailed into the Philippines they were there too. While in the city of Cagayan de Oro they visited a children's home and fell in love with a beautiful little Philippino orphan girl whom they wanted to adopt. The directors of the home were happy about the idea. But the ship was due to leave in less than a week. There was no way possible to get a passport for the child in such a short time. No way from man's point of view perhaps, but not from God's.

After much prayer a letter was drafted to the president asking for his help. It was signed by the ship's director, George Miley and taken personally to the palace of the president.

That very day, 7 August, 1973, the president gave to the *Logos* delegation a note handwritten on official stationery and addressed to the Undersecretary of Foreign Affairs:

'See that the child adopted by one of the members of the delegation of M/V Logos (the library ship) gets his passport before they sail on Friday, Aug 10th.

This will be hand carried by Capt. Paget and/or Dir. George Miley.'

At the bottom of the letter was the scrawled signature of the president.

Three days later the *Logos* sailed with a small child named Emily Dean aboard.

9

Battles on board

A few cigars, not even lit by those who had received them, were enough to fan into flames the fires of resentment that had been smouldering among the ship's engineers for the past two years. The beautifully-wrapped gifts presented to the deck officers at the presidential banquet in the Philippines were found to contain large expensive-looking cigars. As no one on board smoked, the engineers had no use for the cigars, but the thought of being given medallions like the rest of the ship's company, while deck officers were given cigars, rankled. After all, the *Logos* had been asked to provide a list of officers to the president's staff. Obviously, the engineers were not even being considered as officers. Their vital role in the running of the ship was not being accorded proper respect, and consequently their authority was being undermined.

Early in the morning after the presidential banquet, all the engineer officers in full uniform filed into the ship's dining-room and took over a long table which the chief engineer had insisted be reserved for them. The captain already had a table reserved for him and his officers. The chief engineer would have the same for his officers. Head erect, Chief Engineer John Yarr marched determinedly to the head of his table, seated his family and motioned to his officers to seat themselves.

The storm unleashed by this simple action was unbelievable. Many of the non-professional people, not understanding the point the engineers were trying to make, saw things from their own point of view. Reserving seats for engineering officers, whose work would often prevent them from occupying the seats anyway, meant taking seats away from other people because there were not enough seats in the dining-room for the entire ship's company. 'Who do these engineers think they are anyway?' asked some of the people. 'Why should they reserve seats for themselves and leave the rest of us to scramble around as best we can for what is left?' Others expressed impatience or disgust at what they saw only as a childish display of pride.

Ministry leaders realised that this kind of power play had to stop if the ship was going to have any kind of effective work for God. They also realised that they were partly to blame that tensions had escalated to this point.

George Verwer, who would be on the ship for only a few months and then off again for long periods of time in Europe and elsewhere, had quickly realised that he needed someone to work along with him and take over in his absence. In the mid-sixties George had felt very much drawn to a young American named George Miley and had asked him to work closely with him as a typist and helper in India. Verwer recognised Miley's capabilities and began turning more and more responsibility over to him in various areas. That was just the challenge Miley had needed. He became committed heart and soul to India.

When George Verwer had asked him to come to the *Logos* as assistant director, George Miley was not interested. He wanted to stay in India. Verwer, with his own brand of persuasiveness, succeeded in getting him to come to the ship, but he came with great reluctance. His heart was in India and he was just counting the days until

he could return. All the conflicts and tensions he met on
Logos increased his eagerness to get back to the place of
service he loved. Because he saw himself as just a care-
taker in George Verwer's absence, he tended to stand
back from the ship's problems and avoid getting involved
more than necessary.

For all practical purposes this meant that no one was
really in charge. Even when George Verwer was aboard,
he was involved in too many other things to be able to
keep firm leadership. The 'battle of the cigars' brought
matters to a head. George Miley knew that whether he
wanted to get involved or not, the time had come for a
clear and firm stand to be made. Someone had to take
control and straighten out the mess. Frank Dietz, who
was also in ministry leadership, expressed the difficulty in
doing so:

> 'Some of us in the ship ministry wondered whether or not the
> project might go under simply because of the antagonism that
> we often sensed on board. I know George Miley and I at
> times feared to stand up and give morning devotions or even
> to make announcements—something, of course, we had to
> overcome. But we felt very intimidated, mainly because we
> were in such a new thing—a ministry we didn't know any-
> thing about. Often some of the professional seamen would
> come to us and back us into a corner, as they would tell us we
> basically didn't know anything about ships. That, of course,
> was true. We didn't know how ships functioned. We didn't
> know how the ministry should be carried out. We didn't
> know how the relationship between director and captain
> should be worked out.'

George Miley called together the entire ship's company
for a meeting that evening to try to sort things out. It was
a lively meeting with people heatedly giving vent to their
emotions, criticising, arguing, and shouting. An engineer
stood up in one corner and began to express his views. In
another corner a deckman shot up and snapped loudly,
'Stop talking all this rubbish!' Whatever faults people may
have had, suppressing their feelings did not appear to be
one of them.

Into this atmosphere, bristling with tension from injured pride, callous accusations, suspicion, bitterness, disgust, impatience and a host of other things, George Miley stepped forward to take control. Instead of denouncing people for their immature and unspiritual actions, he gently explained to the ship's company the position of engineers on a ship—the training and expertise they had, their importance and their status as officers on the same level as deck officers. He made very clear to the ship people that they should give engineer officers the respect due their position.

This very clear word was followed by the reading of a parable of Jesus recorded in Luke 14:7–11:

> 'When he noticed how the guests picked the places of honour at the table, he told them this parable: "When someone invites you to a wedding feast, do not take the place of honour, for a person more distinguished than you may have been invited. If so, the host who invited both of you will come and say to you, 'Give this man your seat.' Then, humiliated, you will have to take the least important place. But when you are invited, take the lowest place, so that when your host comes, he will say to you, 'Friend, move up to a better place.' Then you will be honoured in the presence of all your fellow guests. For everyone who exalts himself will be humbled, and he who humbles himself will be exalted." '

Very clearly, very simply, George Miley underlined the quality God is looking for in a person; not egotism and pride that fights for recognition but a humble, loving spirit that is willing to let other people receive praise and honour.

Even before the meeting, Mike Poynor, John Yarr, and one or two other engineers had met to discuss the whole business of the dining-room table and had concluded that it was totally unnecessary and was even an embarrassment. They agreed that the way the engineers were treated was not right, but felt this was not the way to rectify the situation.

John Yarr, quick to take action to try to right a wrong, was equally open in admitting faults. Revealing both courage and humility, he stood before the ship's company the following morning and confessed that the engineers had not acted in a godly manner. They deeply regretted this and would return to their previous seating arrangements.

On the following day, George Miley had a meeting with Bjørn and John to discuss the situation and try to work out some ways to resolve it. Both Bjørn and John openly confessed to wrong reactions in their dealings with one another and with other officers. Together they prayed that God would forgive them and help them in the future to deal with matters in a way that would please God.

God was showing the ship that he was not looking for perfect people—no one would qualify in that case—but for people who would let him work in their lives to develop his character in them. It took strong, determined men to pioneer a project like the ship, but those very qualities needed to be tempered by the spirit of God in order to produce strong, steadfast men of God.

The results of the affair were felt by everyone on board. Not just the easing of tension between deck and engineer officers. (Many non-crew people had hardly been aware of the existence of such tension.) But relief in sensing that finally the spiritual leaders were in charge of the ship—not the engine room or the deck, but the overall operations of the ship. Instead of everyone airing his own opinion about where the ship should go, what it should sell, and what it should do, there was someone to give clear and firm spiritual guidance. From this time onward, the people on the ship felt that they were beginning to fulfil the task for which the *Logos* had been bought. It was this which made the incident with the cigars so important.

As for George Miley himself, this appeared to be a turning point in his attitude toward the ship. Like it or not, he was fully involved with it now. With the involvement came a growing sense of commitment to the ship

BATTLES ON BOARD 105

ministry, a commitment that was strengthened as he began to see more and more of the potential of the *Logos* as a tool in God's hands.

From the Philippines the ship moved on to Manado, Indonesia. The programme in the Philippines had been very busy. The crew was understaffed and overworked, fighting constantly to keep old equipment, especially the generators, in working condition. Tension on board had taken its toll as well. Many people were drained emotionally and physically. The voyage was too short to offer much opportunity for rest and recovery of energy. Frank Dietz, wrote in his diary, 'How much more can we take?'

The answer was, 'A lot more.' Manado proved to be one of the busiest ports the *Logos* had yet experienced. Mike Wiltshire, still the one and only line-up man, had gone ahead to plan the programme and to order books in Indonesian so they would be waiting for the ship. Nothing had been heard from him, so the ship did not know what to expect when they arrived in Manado.

Mike had done his job very well, they found out when they got to Manado, but, as it turned out, not well enough. That was not his fault. No one could have anticipated the response. Two tons of Indonesian literature had been shipped to Manado for the visit. This was presumed to be enough to last for the four Indonesian ports which would be visited. A great miscalculation. Well before the end of the two-week visit to the first port, the exhibition was running out of Christian books, especially Bibles and song-books. These were being airfreighted from the Indonesian island of Java where they had sat for years on the shelves. Indonesia had plenty of Christian literature. The bottleneck was distribution. People were hungry for God's word. When the airfreighted cartons of Bibles arrived, the demand was so great that they were opened right on the quayside. As quickly as the Bibles could be pulled out of the cartons, they were sold.

Christian hymn-books too were greatly in demand. Churches were so short of these that in the services someone would stand and read the first line of a hymn. The congregation would respond by singing that line. The second line would be read quickly and clearly, and the congregation would sing that line. And so on. Quite understandably the people were eager to get song-books.

One Indonesian woman gave a stirring testimony of how she had come to know Jesus Christ through a book she had bought on the *Logos*. Later it was discovered that very book had been in her church bookshop but she had never seen it. The *Logos* had actually bought it from the church bookshop in order to sell it on the ship.

Carol Ann Poynor remembers going out door-to-door with Hanna, George Miley's wife. 'We'd come home,' she said, 'with chickens, mangos and rabbits, because people didn't have money.'

'We went to a Catholic seminary and the priest told the boys they could each choose a book. Each of them solemnly chose *The Knowledge of the Holy* by A W Tozer. Then the senior priest went away. As soon as he did, the young seminarians all rushed to grab a book on sex, love and marriage and stick it hastily in their robes. We didn't have enough copies, so Hanna ran out quickly to the van to get more. When she came back, the senior priest had returned and the boys had somehow lost all interest in the book.'

A two-day conference scheduled on the ship for pastors was so well received that it was extended for a third day. Even that wasn't enough for the pastors. They asked if another pastors' conference could be held. Anticipating more participants than the eighty or ninety who could be squeezed into the dining-room of the *Logos*, the pastors rented a building ashore and publicised the meetings on the radio. More than 400 came to the three-day conference. From every denomination they came. Thinking of the many divisions among the churches, one delegate could hardly believe it. 'Nothing like this has ever happened here before!' he exclaimed.

Three international rallies held in an open field were attended by more than 20,000 people. Hundreds of people decided to turn to Christ or, if they had already made that decision, to renew their commitment to him.

The ship was swamped with volunteers. Some 120 Indonesians helped out in various kinds of practical work. Some of them, as they joined *Logos* teams in house-to-house and street evangelism, talked to people about Jesus Christ for the first time in their lives.

Four teams from the ship went inland on short evangelistic trips into the villages. Taking a very clear lead in this and in all forms of evangelism were the Indian men aboard the *Logos*. A well-known Indonesian evangelist cancelled trips to the Philippines and to Korea in order to be able to work along with the *Logos* in its outreach. Werner Jahnke, a German missionary, brought a team of four Indonesians from a Bible school in Java to help as well. The deep involvement of so many Indonesian Christians was invaluable.

In 1987, fifteen years later, Lloyd Nicholas, who was by then Programme Co-ordinator for the ministry of OM ships, made a survey trip to Indonesia and visited Manado. There he met quite a number of people who told him they had become Christians during the visit of the *Logos* in 1972. These and other Christians said that the start of church growth in that area could be linked directly to the visit of the *Logos*. Lloyd was amazed at the life of the churches of Manado. On a Sunday the streets would be full of people streaming to church, Bibles tucked under their arms. After the church services, one could drive down the streets and see many little groups sitting in the open-style tropical houses and poring over the Bible together. 'I've never seen anything like it,' commented Lloyd.

The incredible responsiveness of the Indonesians had been a dramatic example of God at work. Getting ready

to sail from Manado to the next Indonesian port, the
Logos people were riding high on a crest of spiritual and
emotional elation. What more strategic time could the
forces of evil choose to strike a blow? And what better
avenue than through the ship officers who so dearly
wanted to follow God wholeheartedly yet kept getting
caught up in their own weaknesses?

Non-crew members of the ship may have assumed that,
after the resolving of the cigar incident, all tensions
between the deck officers and the engineers had disappeared, but that was not true. Resolving problems in
human relationships is generally a long process requiring
persistent effort.

'Many times Bjørn sat in our cabin sharing with John
his anxiety over running the *Logos*,' wrote John's wife.
'Many cups of coffee were consumed as they discussed the
problem of handling so many very young new sea-goers.'

In spite of this deep desire to see everything running
smoothly and efficiently, points of conflict continued to
arise.

One of the grievances of the engineers was that the
deck officers often would not inform them when the
engines were no longer needed, although this would be
standard procedure on other ships. Engineers would
remain needlessly on standby long after the deckmen had
finished and left. Engineers naturally felt this was not
right.

On this occasion the ship was due to sail from Manado
early in the morning around six o'clock. At four a.m. the
engineers had the engines ready. At five a.m. they tested
the steering gear and other things. Afterwards they were
put on half-hour notice, meaning that at any time with a
half hour's notice the engines should be set to go. They
waited. Nothing happened. No orders, no explanation,
nothing. Hour after hour passed. Indignant that his engineers had to remain on alert hour after hour, the chief
engineer stormed up to the bridge, and demanded to

know what was going on. Bjørn, on the defensive, replied
that it was not his fault. He had been expecting the pilot
since early morning. An angry exchange of words followed. Finally, as John turned to leave, he told the captain that he could have the engines when he, John, said
so.

'The pilot may be arriving at any time,' Bjørn reminded
him.

'That's fine, but he won't get any engines,' was John's
parting shot.

Greatly upset, Bjørn went to talk with George Miley
about the situation. Even before the pilot finally showed
up about eleven o'clock that evening, George Miley
decided to drop into the engine room to see what would
happen. Only one person was there, the young engineer
on watch. They had a good talk, a talk which was abruptly
ended by a command for the engines to stand by. The bell
kept ringing and ringing, but the young engineer made no
move to answer it. Leaning over to Miley, he informed
him, 'The chief has given orders that he will answer the
command tonight.'

Seconds later John burst into the engine room where he
studiously ignored the loud ringing of the bell. The captain called down, but no one moved to take the call. A
few minutes later, Captain Kristiansen stalked in and
asked sarcastically whether or not he should send the pilot
away. Heated words followed.

Mike Poynor, who was just going to bed because he had
the four to eight o'clock watch, heard the continuous
ringing of the bell and thought something must be wrong
in the engine room. Getting up and pulling his clothes
back on, he went down to the engine room to investigate.
In his quiet, sensible way he took in the whole situation
and defused it by commenting matter-of-factly, 'Well,
we've been waiting all day. Why don't we get going?'

Dead silence. Then John reached for the signal and
moved it to standby position. Bjørn announced that

because he was a Christian he would now go up and take the ship out. The crisis was past.

But that was not the end of the story. On the following day Bjørn wrote in his diary, 'Had a good time with John and we prayed together.'

It should come as no surprise to find conflicts arising on the ship. Conflicts are a normal part of life, even for deeply-committed Christians. What was amazing was that after such strong clashes, God could bring the people involved to a place of forgiveness and continue to develop in them a deep love for one another.

John and Bjørn had one more dramatic meeting. After fulfilling his commitment on the *Logos*, John returned to Sydney, Australia, where he began a regular prayer meeting in his home and challenging people to go to work on the *Logos* and in other OM fields. Bjørn, after leaving *Logos*, served as chief officer on a passenger ship which called in at Australia. On this occasion he found John waiting for him on the quayside. When the two men met, they threw their arms around each other. So great was their emotion that they stood there and cried.

10

Changes on the bridge

The incredible responsiveness of the Indonesian people to the word of God was seen throughout the rest of the ship's stay there. Every port was as busy as Manado had been, yet all the Bibles on the *Logos* had long since been sold. Halfway through the visit to Ambon, a consignment of 470 Bibles and 1,200 New Testaments arrived from Java. Within forty-eight hours they were all gone.

There was a steady flow of people who wanted to know how to become a real Christian, not just in name but in a personal way. A group of theological students who were helping in evangelism realised that they themselves had not received this gift of personal salvation, and prayed in repentance and faith with their team-mates from the *Logos*.

The third port in Indonesia was Kupang on the island of Timor, where revival had begun in Indonesia a few years earlier. Since the *Logos* had only one line-up man and he had his hands full with the other ports, the leaders decided to send a telegram to the Bible Society there, explaining what the ship was and asking the Bible Society to prepare a programme. From there on the programme was left entirely in the hands of the local Christians in the

Bible Society. They did an excellent job, probably better than someone from the ship could have done.

During the time in Kupang a Christian anthropologist was invited to speak to the ship's people. He described his investigation to try to find out why the revival in Indonesia had died out. His conclusion was that there were three basic reasons; lack of morals, desire for material things and pride. These were three of the main things that the *Logos* leaders were preaching against in pastors' conferences and in other believers' meetings.

One day some of the men working out on the deck of the ship looked up to see a procession heading toward the ship. That in itself was not unusual; groups of people were always streaming toward the ship. What made this procession different was that the people were leading along a bull. When they arrived at the newly-built jetty, they came to a halt. Just beside the main pillar supporting the jetty, the men dug a hole. This done, they proceeded to kill the bull, cut off its head, lay it carefully in the hole and cover it with earth. By this time quite a crowd had gathered on the deck of the ship to stare in macabre fascination at the strange ritual, wondering what it all meant. Afterwards they learned that the Indonesians they had been watching were animists sacrificing a bull so that the jetty might become 'strong as a bull'. For *Logos* personnel it was a stark reminder of how much these people needed to hear of the one true God.

An entirely different kind of event also took place in Indonesia. Bernhard Erne, the bos'un, had been working with a couple of his deckmen, Ebbo Buurma and Urs Baumgartner. The hull of the ship down near the waterline needed to be repainted. To do this, the men used a small work-boat. As they worked and talked, someone suggested it would be fun to go for a sail in the little boat some time. So one lunchtime they set off. Ebbo remembers:

'We rigged up the sail and shot away from the *Logos* at tremendous speed into what we thought was a bay. It wasn't.

It was two islands that were overlapping each other from our point of view.

'We sailed only about ten minutes and then decided to return to the *Logos*. We turned the boat around so we had the full wind blowing in our sails, but the boat didn't move forward. It went backwards. We took the oars and rowed like mad, but the boat kept going backwards. We realised we were in a very narrow strait with an enormous current pushing us out into the open sea.

'So we began to row to one of the islands. When we got close, we discovered there were all kinds of big rocks sitting just under the water line. Just at that moment we saw a small shark swim under the boat in the clear water. That made us a bit nervous as we tried to row around the rocks.

'All of a sudden I caught sight of a huge fin sticking up out of the water. I got such a shock I started rowing twice as fast and screamed, "A shark!" Urs fell backwards in the boat. Bernhard, who was at the rudder, jumped up and grabbed the hook, ready to attack the shark before he could attack us. He was enormous, at least five metres long. Praise God, he disappeared, but we were so shocked.

'We moved out into deeper water. We had an anchor with us and a long rope, so we threw the anchor into the water and just sat there. We crawled under the sail and waited to see if the current would change.

'After about four hours under that sail, we noticed that the water level had dropped considerably and a jetty was sticking out from the other island not far from us. It had been under water earlier.

'We rowed behind the jetty and saw some Indonesian men. We shouted to them and they came, but they didn't go into the water, because of the dangerous fish. We threw them a rope and they pulled us on shore.

'About eleven o'clock that evening they indicated we should get into the boats. Our boat was attached to theirs. When we got close to the ship, we gave them our deck-knives as presents and told them they could go while we rowed the rest of the way. We could hear talking on the ship as we came near. There was great confusion and fear because no one knew where we were or what had happened to us. Out of the dark someone shouted, "Here they are!" We thought we could sneak aboard quietly, but the whole ship was waiting for us.'

From Indonesia the *Logos* sailed to Singapore and then on to Cochin. On the voyage, Bjørn Kristiansen informed George Miley that he wanted to leave the ship in Cochin.

The announcement was nothing new. Bjørn had often declared he wanted to leave but had always yielded to pressure by the leaders to stay. He had never wanted the job as captain in the first place. He had taken it only because there was no one else. Being captain on a ship with only a handful of experienced seamen among a crowd of landlubbers was enough to try the soul of any man. Add to that the widely different backgrounds and training of these few professionals. Then toss in the fact that the ship was trying to accommodate a ministry, but still no one knew exactly what that ministry was or how it should function, much less how it should fit into the structure of ship life. All these things were still being worked out. Top all this with the realisation that Bjørn, a relatively new Christian, had naïvely come to the ship expecting to find it staffed with mature, godly people whose lives would be an example to everyone.

The remarkable thing about Bjørn was not that he wanted to escape from it all. That was understandable. The remarkable thing was that in spite of all the pressures, in spite of his oft-repeated desire to leave, he stuck to his post. He was where God had put him and there he would stay until God released him and sent him on somewhere else.

This time when Bjørn brought up the matter, George Miley sensed that perhaps the time had come for him to be released.

'If you feel you should go,' George told him, 'then go. If God wants the *Logos* to continue, he'll provide another captain. If he doesn't, we'll just stay where we are. It's as simple as that.'

When the ship arrived in Cochin, Bjørn did leave. His departure marked the end of an era for the *Logos*. The pioneering days were past. The time had come for consolidation. Bjørn Kristiansen had been God's man in God's place at God's time to take the ship through those turbulent days of charting a course into the unknown. Now it was time for a very different type of man to take over the helm.

Waiting on the quayside as the ship sailed into Cochin was Captain Paget.

George Herbert Paget, a retired British captain, had been at sea all his life, most of the time around India. Another British captain had this to say about him:

'Often when I met various Christians around ports of India, they would ask, "Do you know Captain Paget?" He was a man well-known at sea and well-known for his faith and trust in the Lord. I think perhaps the best testimony to his life I ever heard came from a non-Christian, a Hindu. When I was taking an examination in Bombay, I palled up with a young Indian officer because our names came together on the examination list. The following Sunday I went along to Captain Paget's ship, because we were to go to church together. Going up the gangway, I met my friend of the previous week.

"'So they've appointed you here," I commented. "What do you think of the ship?"

"'Oh, this is a good ship to be on," he said. "It's good to be with Holy Paget. The superintendents never bother you when you're on Holy Paget's ship. They know that he does everything well. And besides, they don't like his big black Bible that he reads all the time."

'That, coming from a Hindu, was to me a wonderful testimony of a man whose life was stable, straight, trusted by even non-Christian directors and superintendents.'

Captain Paget had been asked to relieve Bjørn Kristiansen the previous year when Bjørn had taken leave to get married. Paget had been somewhat sceptical of the *Logos*, but he had agreed to come for a few months anyway. During those three and a half months he had grown to love the *Logos* and her people. That was why he was on the quayside in Cochin. He had come only to visit the ship, but with a little persuasion he was induced to take over as captain of the ship again.

A white-haired man in a black beret and scruffy clothes, he shuffled around the ship, sometimes giving the impression of a doddering old man. That impression was completely false. Captain Paget was an old experienced seahand, fully aware of everything happening on his ship, completely in control. He knew all the tricks, so no one could put anything over on him, but he trusted his men and left them free to get on with the job, letting them know he was always available if they wanted help.

Whenever Indian port officials came on board the *Logos* and learned that Paget was captain, an immediate difference was apparent in their attitudes. Pilots coming on board would go up to the bridge, catch sight of the old, white-haired captain, suddenly snap to attention and salute. 'Good morning, Captain Paget, sir. Do you remember me, sir? I was a junior on one of your ships at such-and-such a time . . . ' Hardly an Indian official came on the ship who did not know 'Holy Paget'—know him, respect him and love him.

As an older man, more detached from the rest of the ship, Paget gave the ship the sense of stability that it needed. He would mumble and grumble out of the side of his mouth, but really he loved it on the ship. And he got along well with everybody. The Indians, especially, would always be up in his cabin.

He had an inexhaustible fund of jokes and he loved to visit cabins of families, chatting and telling his jokes. Invariably, he would be rewarded with tea and cake. He developed an infallible instinct for turning up at the cabin of the wife who had just had her weekly turn at baking in the ship's galley.

In the autumn of 1972, with a new captain at the helm, the time for the change-over of personnel came around again. People on the ship began to view this annual event as the end of one ship year and the beginning of the next. As before, the ship steamed into the Gulf to be as close as possible to Europe.

Since the visit in the Gulf had gone so well the previous year, people on the ship were encouraged to be somewhat bolder this time. In Dubai when the censor came to check the books on the exhibition, he saw some Christian ones. On the previous visit no Christian books had been displayed publicly; they were kept behind the scenes and only given out privately to Christians. The book exhibition staff wondered what the censor would say about the Christian books. He said nothing. Wanting to clarify the situation, to make sure they were doing nothing illegal, exhibition leaders questioned him about the books. His response was that the *Logos* could not give out Christian literature; that would be propaganda. Nothing could be put into the hands of local people. However, the people themselves could pick up anything that was offered in the exhibition. In that case the local people would be taking the initiative, so it would not be considered propaganda.

How to make the most effective use of a situation like that was a challenge! The answer the book exhibition workers came up with was to set up a table offering a free book as a premium for any purchase on the exhibition. On the table were two selections from which to choose: a book of Arabic poetry or a beautiful edition of a Christian book in Arabic. The stock of Christian books dwindled rapidly while the poetry remained virtually undisturbed.

Carol Ann Poynor, working at the cash desk late one night, was petrified when suddenly confronted by a man in flowing robes with bands of bullets strapped across his chest. Just behind him were two other men.

'A friend of mine got a book on how to become a Christian. I want one too,' he announced.

Trying to marshall her paralysed wits, Carol Ann stammered, 'Well, we've got these two books here. This is a poetry book and this is a Christian book. If you'd like the Christian book, you can take it.'

He took it.

From Dubai, the ship moved on to Abadan, in Iran, where the change-over of personnel took place. Then on to Doha, in Qatar. Almost all the ministry here was focused on the expatriate community. Many teams went to church meetings among various groups, particularly among the Indians. Giovanni Ammirabile, an Italian, had a special concern for the Catholic priests in the area, most of whom were Italian or Spanish, and he would often go and talk with them.

When the ship had come into Doha, it had come at the invitation of the Minister of Information, who was willing to 'stick his neck out' and take the risk of sponsoring the ship. He did it with the understanding that no Christian books would be sold. Peter Holmes, who had been in charge of line-up, had agreed. This fact was made very clear to the entire ship's company.

Some people, however, chafed at the restriction. How could they be in the heart of Islamic territory and not try to do something to let the people know about Jesus Christ? Surely something could be done if it were done very discreetly. A team of two women going out to sell educational books door-to-door stuck a couple of Christian books at the very bottom of their book bags, just in case someone indicated a special interest. Someone did.

At one house the woman who received the *Logos* women was very interested, looking first at the books and then getting into conversation. She ended up buying one of the Christian books as well as some educational ones. Delighted with her purchases, she showed them to her husband when he came home at midday and told him all about the visit. The husband, as it turned out, was the Minister of Information. And he definitely did not share his wife's delight. Getting on the phone immediately, he angrily delivered an ultimatum to the ship. It must leave by five o'clock that evening.

Greatly shaken by the affair, the ship's leaders went to the Minister and apologised profusely. The incident had happened without their knowledge. They deeply regretted the breach of trust and assured the minister that such a thing would not happen again if the ship were allowed to remain.

The Minister, however, would relent only to the extent of allowing the ship to remain a few hours longer than the original deadline. A vastly subdued ship, and two conscience-stricken women, who would never again disobey specific orders, left the Gulf for India and points beyond.

11

Country at war

The *Logos* gleamed white in the sun as she worked her way up the winding course of the Saigon River in Vietnam. Most of her people, if they were not actively involved in running the ship or tied down to some other job, were out on the deck, eager to see as much as possible of this war-torn country that had been so long in the news. The banks of the river, which had been scorched to the earth to eliminate possible hiding-places for enemy soldiers, had begun to sprout again with fresh vegetation, but the impression of bleak flatness remained. The occasional sight of the burned-out shell of a tank or an army truck added more grim reminders that this was a country at war.

Vietnam was at that time a country long mutilated by fighting, its wounds lying open, bleeding. Its young people had grown up never knowing anything but war. First there was fighting under the French occupation when the country was part of Indo-China. The French withdrew, only to be followed by Communist insurgents known as the Viet Cong. American forces poured onto the scene to try to prevent Communist forces engulfing the country. For years they supported the tottering government of South Vietnam until the frustrations of a

stalemate and the fear of a possible defeat led to the
withdrawal of the troops. Vietnam lay waiting for the
inevitable to happen.

In the late afternoon of 2 August 1974, the *Logos*
reached Saigon, slipping quietly into a berth in the heart
of a city bustling with activity and largely unaware of the
little ship that had come to bring a message of peace and
hope.

It had been a long day filled with new sights and impressions that did little to ease the sense of apprehension felt
by the *Logos* people as they went into a war zone.
Repeated reports had assured them that there was no
danger for them in Saigon for the time being. With this
comforting thought they settled down for their first night
in Vietnam. Suddenly a loud explosion reverberated
throughout the ship, startling everyone into an instant and
uneasy wakefulness. A couple of minutes later there was
another deafening bang, followed by a series of others at
regular intervals. Then silence. Only the normal sounds of
the ship's generators. Eventually the ship's company settled down to an uneasy sleep again, sensing that nothing
dreadful was going to happen after all.

The following morning they learned this was just a
normal routine operation carried out every night in the
Saigon River. At low tide, in the middle of the night,
security police would check all ships in the river, going
under water to make sure that no mines had been
attached to the bottom of the ships. When the police came
up, they would toss depth charges into the water. The
shock waves from these would ensure that any Viet Cong
saboteur who might be lurking under the water would no
longer be in business. The sound effect was like that of a
sledge hammer pounding against a metal drum. For
people inside the ship, the depth charges might cause a
startling disturbance but they caused no harm. No one
had thought to inform the *Logos* people about the practice.

On Tuesday the official opening of the book exhibition took place. Vietnamese soldiers, standing stiffly at attention with their guns upright against their shoulders, formed two columns ending at the foot of the gangway of the *Logos*. A black limousine drew up. From its depths emerged the prime minister of Vietnam. Walking between the two columns of soldiers, he reached the gangway and was escorted aboard by the chief officer of the *Logos*.

When the exhibition was finally opened to the general public, the *Logos* staff were not prepared for the crowds. Seeing the crowd building up just before the opening, some of the staff went out on the quayside and tried to get the people to come in an orderly manner through one little gate, but the press of the crowd made that impossible. The docking area was a large square place jutting out into the river. On either side of it was a road leading to the berth. Between the roads lay water, spanned by narrow steel girders. People began scrambling over the girders in order to reach the ship. Horrified, the book exhibition staff tried to stop them, but that only made matters worse; it brought the danger of people being pushed into the water. What a relief when the day finally came to an end without mishap!

That evening the *Logos* family gathered for a night of prayer. The chaotic and dangerous situation was handed over to God for him to work out in some way. The next day when the Vietnamese came to the book exhibition, they lined up. Basically they did it on their own initiative, though a couple of *Logos* men were there on the quayside to show them where the end of the line was. Long-time residents of Saigon couldn't believe it and kept telling the ship people that they'd never seen Vietnamese line up for anything.

Some time before the arrival of the ship, George Verwer had gone to Vietnam to see if a visit by the ship was feasible. While there, he had gone through a warehouse of Christian literature in Saigon and had seen shelves full of Christian books in Vietnamese, many of which had obviously been sitting there for years.

'Why aren't these books selling?' he asked and then went on, 'We want to sell them on the ship.' When the ship arrived they were taken aboard. During that same advance visit, George had spoken to a group of Vietnamese pastors and introduced them to some of these books in their own language. They'd never seen them.

With such crowds visiting the ship, the supply of Christian literature didn't last long. One of the book exhibition men went to a small shop, the main Christian bookshop in Saigon, and bought more. When these were sold out, he returned for more until he had bought out most of the stock. Many of these books had been on the shelves for years. More than 17,000 Christian books in Vietnamese were sold on the ship during that short visit.

Every day someone from the book exhibition would go to the bank with big bags full of money from the sale of books. This impressive picture was not due, however, so much to big business as to the fact that the local currency was devaluing so fast—seven, eight, sometimes as much as twelve per cent in the course of a single day. Every day when the money was taken to the bank to be changed into dollars, it was worth much less. For some reason the Vietnamese seemed to like to pay in small currency notes, which added significantly to the volume of paper money. One of the book exhibition men, impressed by the tellers in the bank, commented, 'Nowhere, except possibly in Indonesia, have I seen people in banks count money so fast. With incredible speed they could get through huge mountains of notes.'

The book exhibition was only a part of the many varied activities of the ship. The chief officer and the public relations man paid a visit to every cabinet member in the government, talking about the ship, describing their own personal experiences with Jesus Christ and presenting each official who had not already received it a beautiful copy of the *Living Bible*. One top-ranking official who had been presented with a Bible sent a message to the ship two days later asking if they would send him another Bible. He'd been reading the Bible in his office and he'd never read anything like it. He wanted to have another one for his home so he could read it there as well. The president of Vietnam, who was unable to visit the ship, sent for a list of the books available so that he could select some of them. Among those he bought was *How To Win over Worry* by John Haggai.

In the months before the arrival of the ship, the line-up men, Peter Conlan and a Canadian named Warwick Cooper, had gone ahead to Saigon to make arrangements. There they had invited local pastors, other Vietnamese Christian leaders and missionaries to form a committee and work with them in trying to plan a programme that would best fit the needs of the Vietnamese people. The Christian leaders entered into the task with great enthusiasm. Peter then moved on to the next port of call, leaving his less experienced colleague to negotiate in a language he didn't understand. His translator would sometimes get so involved that he would pause only occasionally to give Warwick the gist of what was going on. A frustrating experience for the man who was ultimately responsible for it all! Government officials were very co-operative. As a matter of fact, twenty high-ranking government officials spent two entire mornings working with the committee to help in obtaining all the necessary permissions.

As usual, one of the major elements of the programme planned by the committee was meetings. There were meetings on board the ship: special dinners or receptions for such widely varying groups as bank officials, Christian leaders, doctors, and Indian businessmen; conferences for pastors, missionaries, young people, new Christians; and tours for school groups. On shore there were meetings as well; teams of *Logos* people visited the university, schools, orphanages, hospitals, and churches. Officers and young people alike would talk about life aboard ship and then go on to share some of their own personal experiences with Jesus Christ. Officers who were experts in their field often felt out of their element when facing an audience. Most of the young people too had never spoken in public before joining the ship. Their nervousness was often apparent as their voices shook and they stumbled over words. Yet their sincerity was obvious and somehow quite moving. These were not polished professionals rattling off pious-sounding religious phrases. They were ordinary people speaking about something that was real to them, and that fact communicated itself to the hearers, creating in them a yearning for the same experience of meaning, purpose and direction in life. Many people were able to find it.

When the teams went to a church, they would usually take along a selection of Christian books to offer to the people. As Anneli Dietz, a young Finnish woman, was taking care of a book table after a church service, a young Vietnamese girl shyly approached her, wanting to know more about the ship. Anneli chatted for a while with her and casually invited her to come to the ship sometime. A few days later she showed up at a most inconvenient time just before lunch. Anneli welcomed her and took her around to show her the ship, but it was a hasty tour because Anneli was very conscious of the fast-approaching lunch-hour. Suddenly the girl dropped her conversation about the ship and said bluntly, 'What I'm really interested in is Jesus Christ.'

Ashamed at her own behaviour, Anneli hurried off to get another Finnish woman who could communicate better because she knew French. The two of them spent a long time with the Vietnamese girl, telling her what Jesus had done for her and describing the kind of life he offered, a life free from guilt and full of meaning but also

full of responsibility. The girl finally prayed and committed her life to Jesus Christ.

Every evening an evangelistic rally was held on the
quay beside the ship. The Pocket Testament League provided the equipment to show Moody Science films—films
about science but with a Christian message. Great crowds
would come to the ship in the evening and, since it got
dark shortly after six o'clock, these films could be shown
outdoors, using the side of the ship as a huge screen easily
visible to everyone. For two or three hours films were
shown, then local Christians explained more fully the
message in the films and a number of people made
decisions to follow Christ. These new Christians were
invited to weekly meetings that had been set up for the
time after the ship had left. These meetings offered further teaching in the Christian faith.

Every visitor to the *Logos* was given a Gospel and a
specially-printed Vietnamese tract entitled *What is the
Logos?* Many other tracts containing the message of
Christ were passed out by *Logos* people on street corners
and in busy markets. Two special tract weekends were
organised with large groups of *Logos* people joining local
Christians in going out to distribute tracts together. This
was one way *Logos* people could communicate the message without the assistance of translators.

Carol Ann Poynor used to go out every morning with a
couple of other *Logos* women to the local market. The
main street of Saigon ran right along the river beside the
ship. *Logos* people had only to cross the dock area to this
street and turn left. There it was—the large open-air
market teeming with activity. You could buy anything you
wanted there: uniforms—Viet Cong, French, American,
you name it; black-market coffee, radios, just about anything available in the United States. Carol Ann and her
colleagues took 'Gospel packets' to sell. Carol Ann,
describing the experience, said, 'These packets were supposed to sell for fifty dong. But Vietnamese is a tonal

language and I have trouble with tones. I found out I had been trying to sell them for five hundred dong instead of fifty. Anyway, we sold a lot of these packets.'

In all, some 500,000 pieces of Christian literature, from tracts to booklets and complete Gospels, all donated by local Christian organisations, were put into the hands of Saigonese people.

During the last week of their stay a team from the *Logos* was able to fly up to Phnom Penh in Cambodia, a country that was in the middle of its own war. It was a privilege never to be forgotten, for Cambodia at that time was experiencing an unprecedented time of spiritual openness with thousands of people, including Buddhist monks, turning to Christ. The main purpose of the *Logos* team's visit was to hold a five-day training conference for Christian young people with morning sessions on such topics as the Bible, prayer, love, discipleship, and evangelism. Afternoons provided an opportunity for practical experience in tract distribution, selling of Scripture portions and open-air preaching. 'At the first meeting,' wrote George Miley, 'four Buddhist monks showed up in their flowing robes. On the second day of the conference, which was not evangelistic, one of the monks received Christ. Monks are asking for Bible studies. We heard of another monk who had been converted and remained in his Pagoda witnessing to other monks. "I'm a monk for Jesus," he said.'

Though the programme was intense, it was not all work for the *Logos* people. There were times of relaxation as well. Many were invited to the homes of local Christians, missionaries, and other warm-hearted people. The local committee that had organised the *Logos* visit arranged sightseeing tours for them. Buses came to the ship to pick up anyone who was not working at the time and take them to various places of interest like the factories where beautiful lacquered pictures were made from crushed eggshells or where silk weaving was done. Sandbags lining the streets again reminded the *Logos* people that a war was going on. Not that they were likely to forget it. The sound of distant sporadic gunfire was common. And garlanded trucks carrying the bodies of soldiers who had been killed on the battlefield were a daily sight in Saigon. As the bus carrying the *Logos* company passed the sandbags, the tour guide kindly pointed out that the only sandbags one need worry about were those where the sand was pouring out. That meant a bullet had hit there.

By the time the visit of the *Logos* drew to a close, the whole city of Saigon was talking about the ship and the message it had presented. Extensive coverage on radio and television and in newspapers, posters, meetings, personal contacts, the attraction of the book exhibition—all had combined to make the *Logos* the event of the day. Reginald Reimer, a missionary who had worked in Vietnam for many years, wrote, 'The gospel became a public issue to a greater extent than it ever was before.' People were incredibly open to the message of Jesus Christ and many decided to accept that message and turn their lives over to Christ.

The local Christian community had been knit together in an unusually close bond as Christians of various ages and groups had worked together and many made sacrifices to make the visit of the *Logos* a success. The ship had brought this small minority to the attention of the general public in a dynamic and favourable way, giving the church a new sense of self-identity and the confidence to reach out more to the people around them.

And the visit had enriched the lives of both Vietnamese and *Logos* people as they were able to get to know one another and have their eyes and hearts opened to a world outside that of their previous experience. The men and women from the *Logos* had found the Vietnamese incredibly generous and loving.

On the last evening the *Logos* was in port, a group of Vietnamese ladies came aboard and prepared a delicious

MV *Umanak* — built in 1949, sailed the North Sea between Denmark and Greenland, and later became MV *Logos*. (Copenhagen, Denmark: October, 1970).

West-African visitors to the first Book Exhibition on board the *Logos*.

George Miley, Director of the *Logos*, speaking at one of the first conferences for pastors, in India, held in the ship's dining-room.

Many influential guests were welcomed aboard: (above) The first captain of the *Logos*, Bjorn Kristiansen and Petty Officer Mike Wiltshire, show some books (during the exhibition in Bangkok, Thailand, June, 1970) to some distinguished visitors. Prince Mikaso, heir to the Japanese throne, during his visit to the ship in June, 1978. (below)

Guatemalan schoolchildren show their happiness during their visit to the *Logos*.

The *Logos* team of workers were greatly helped in their ministry by being able to transport the van on board the ship. Here they unload it in a port in Indonesia.

Millions of books were sold at the Book Exhibitions (above) or were distributed free of charge at special projects (below) in Central and South America.

Captain George Paget and Chief Engineer, Mike Poynor (at right) with the crew of the *Logos* during their visit to Glasgow, Scotland (July, 1976).

The *Logos* was a floating home for all who sailed in her. Here we see one of the cabins for single ladies (on left) and the creche facilities for the small children. (below)

Professional seamen and volunteers from many countries work behind the scenes to keep the work of the *Logos* functioning. (above)
The ship's kitchen and the workshop (below).

The prime minister of Vietnam officially opened the book exhibition when the *Logos* visited Saigon (August, 1974).

One of the two boats of Vietnamese refugees rescued by the *Logos* in the South China Sea. (October, 1980).

During their stay on board,
many friendships were made
between the 93 Vietnamese
boat-people and the *Logos* team.

Chinese officials are welcomed on board during the visit of the *Logos* to Shangai. (April, 1981).

Peter Conlan, one of the officers of the *Logos*, visited the home of some Chinese Christians, two of the many who prayed for the ship's visit to Shanghai.

At the port of Quetzal, Guatemala, a long line of visitors wait to visit the ship.

Guatemalan seminary students and pastors stock up on books from the literature available on the *Logos*.

Some of the crew wait and pray after the *Logos* ran aground in the Beagle Channel on 4th January, 1988.

Abandoning ship — the 139 crew members were evacuated and taken to land in life-boats.

Aimee Wells, 3 years old, daughter of Graham, the director of the *Logos*, waits patiently aboard one of the life-boats.

The *Logos* aground on the rocks — end of one chapter and the begining of another.

Captain Jonathan Stewart.

Dave Thomas, Chief Engineer.

Graham Wells, Director

The committee members of the *Logos* on her last voyage.

Vietnamese meal for everyone on the ship. The next day, 27 August, as the *Logos* loosened her lines and prepared to leave, hundreds of new-found friends stood on the quayside with tears streaming down their faces as they bid farewell. As the ship pulled away, the people on shore began singing a hymn. From the *Logos* came another in response.

Eight months later Saigon fell to the Communist forces. Many people who had come aboard the *Logos*, including pastors and government officials, lost their lives. And many others went through unimaginable hardship and suffering.

In May 1987, Peter Conlan returned to Saigon (now Ho Chi Minh City). There he discovered that the *Logos* is still fondly remembered by many people. Visiting the Saigon Library one morning, he noticed a number of books from the West.

'Where did these books come from?' he asked.

'Oh, there was a book ship called *Logos* that came here in 1974 . . .'

12

Not without danger

In her seventeen years of ministry, the *Logos* was remark-
ably free of serious accidents. Partly, this can be
explained by the very high standards of safety insisted
upon by the staff and crew. But people on the ship were
always conscious of the hundreds of prayer partners
around the world, continually praying for them and asking God to keep them from danger.

Occasionally, however, God did allow the *Logos*
people to learn through difficulty and even danger. In
December 1975, as the *Logos* steamed into the port of
Istanbul in Turkey, she collided with a ferry boat that
ignored the fact that the *Logos* had the right of way and
tried to cross in front of her when there was not room to
do so.

Manfred Schaller, standing on the bow of the *Logos* to
watch her come into port, remembers watching the two
ships come closer and closer and thinking, 'This can't be
happening. This is God's ship. There couldn't be an accident.' Several passengers on the ferry panicked and
jumped into the water seconds before the jolt that
brought both ships to an abrupt halt. The ferry had been
hit broadside just behind her engine room. Because the
Logos was moving very slowly, the damage to the ferry

was only to her wooden superstructure above water. She was still floating upright and in no danger of sinking.

The crew of the *Logos* immediately threw life-jackets to the ferry passengers who had jumped into the water. A motor boat in the vicinity came to the scene and pulled them out of the water. No one received any injury. However, this did not prevent the ferry owner claiming damages.

Because Islamic Turkey was such a sensitive place in respect to Christianity, the approach of the *Logos* was very low key, with people depending upon personal conversation for opportunities to share about Jesus Christ. Language classes and cultural evenings were set up as a way of making natural contacts with Turks and forming friendships. Two events, however, stand out from that visit to Turkey.

Frank Fortunato, an American responsible for the music ministry of the ship, had been away and returned to the ship on New Year's Day. He was rather taken aback to see posters and banners publicising a concert to be given by the *Logos* choir with Frank Fortunato as director, an event sponsored by a major newspaper. A great opportunity with one drawback. There was no *Logos* choir!

Frank rose to the challenge. What else could he do? With three working days at his disposal, he planned a concert and put together a thirty-voice choir, spending many hours practising with them. To prepare enough music to fill the one-and-a-half hour programme in such a short time was out of the question. Something else would have to be added to fill in some of the time. Someone suggested the idea of cultural acts. About thirty nationalities were represented on the ship. Why not ask some of these people to present a folk dance or song that would be typical of their countries? The idea was such a success that it became the basis for a regular *Logos* feature, the International Night, which would prove to be one of the most popular events in a port.

The small auditorium ashore, which seated 300 people, was packed. Among the songs performed by the choir were some with a clear gospel message for anyone who could understand English. Proceeds from the sale of tickets were given to an orphanage. The event was so well received that a repeat performance was given in the ship's dining-room, which was filled to overflowing.

Another memorable event took place on New Year's Eve. Seventy-five local Armenian and Greek believers, along with a few Turkish ones, slipped quietly and unobtrusively onto the ship. The believers were divided up and sent to different cabins for fellowship with *Logos* families. Afterwards they joined with the entire *Logos* company in a long time of prayer and worship to see the old year out and the new one in. For *Logos* people this was a moving moment, as they realised that the small number of Christians meeting with them on the ship represented a large percentage of all the believers in the entire country of Turkey. Several of these Christians expressed the encouragement it was to them to have a community of 142 believers concentrated in one spot in their city for a month.

Meanwhile the legal battle over damages to the ferry dragged on. The *Logos* was obviously not at fault, but to establish that fact would take a long-drawn-out and expensive process, and the *Logos* was not insured. Val Grieve, the British lawyer serving as chairman of the Educational Book Exhibits board, flew down to Istanbul along with another board member. They recommended that the services of a good Turkish lawyer be obtained and that the *Logos* try to settle out of court to cut down time and expenses. These were both done, although it took a long time to reach a settlement. The ferry owners eventually agreed to settle for half their original claim. In the meantime, the Turkish lira was drastically devalued. In the end, the settlement and legal fees amounted to about one-eighth the original estimate.

Why was *Logos* not insured? The answer was the expense. In the five years the ship had sailed up to this point, she would have already had to pay about £80,000 in insurance premiums. The accident, however, brought the question up again for re-evaluation. As the EBE board investigated the insurance situation, this time having a bit more experience in the shipping world and a few more contacts, they found a place to get cheaper rates. The decision was made to get third party coverage that would take care of any damages to another ship plus any expenses incurred by environmental pollution or blocking of a shipping lane. To buy insurance to cover loss of the *Logos* herself was so expensive that the *Logos* could be bought several times over with the premiums that would be paid in just a few years. The EBE board, like many other small ship owners, decided that was not economically feasible.

Soon after the legal wrangling in Turkey finally came to an end, the *Logos* was faced with a problem of a different, more dramatic, kind. She had spent most of 1976 in Europe, and was heading out to Asia again. Her course would take her through the Bay of Biscay, notorious for its storms. Departure from England for Spain that November day was delayed several hours because of heavy winds. After a slight improvement in weather conditions, the decision was made for the *Logos* to set sail on what should have been a two-day voyage. It lasted four days—four long days.

The slight improvement in weather was only a temporary lull before the real storm hit, the worst in eleven years. Forecasts were warning of Force Twelve winds— hurricane strength. Captain Paget, trying to avoid the worst of the storm, turned the ship westward from her course due south. Even so, the waves were estimated as high as sixty feet. 'Standing on the deck with Captain Paget,' said Dave Hicks, who was director at that time, 'there were times when the bow of the ship was down in the trough of the wave and the bridge was even with the crest of the wave.'

For the new recruits who had only been aboard a month or so, this orientation to ship life was rather brutal! Many of the staff—and even the crew—never made it out of their beds at times. The number who showed up in the dining-room at meal-times dwindled to about ten brave souls—or perhaps one should say ten fortunate souls—who found the whole experience exhilarating. In contrast to most adults, however, the children had a grand time. The deck inside the ship as it rolled from side to side made an excellent place to slide.

The ship bobbed up and down like a cork, pitching and rolling violently. Ship bulkheads, straining under the pressure, would creak and groan, sounding as if the ship were in her death throes; hardly a reassuring sound to young people new to ship life. Most people had only one predominant thought—how to get through the interminable hours ahead, feeling those awful never-ending waves of nausea sweeping over them, robbing them of all interest in living.

Not just the people felt the effects of the wild fury of the elements. The ship herself was taking a mighty beating. The offices looked as if a cyclone had struck them. Furniture was overturned, some of it broken. Books were hurled from shelves. Papers were scattered everywhere.

The major disaster area was the hold where the books were stored. New shelves had just been purchased and installed, but they collapsed under the weight of the books. The movements of the ship sent the boxes crashing to the bottom of the hold in chaotic heaps.

The radio officer heard several mayday calls in the course of a few hours—calls coming from small vessels as far as 200 miles away. But for over twenty-four hours the *Logos* was not able to contact George Verwer by radio telephone in England. George lived in dread of receiving word that the *Logos* had gone down, a fear that was not lessened by newscasts about the violence of the storm and reports of ships in distress. A couple of small ships did actually go down or aground in the Bay of Biscay, they learned later.

Eventually the ship was able to get word out through a French relay station and assured George that, apart from some cargo damage, all was well. Through it all Captain Paget remained steady and confident. If the ship was ever in actual danger, he never gave away the fact. His calmness was a tower of strength to the entire ship.

The winds finally died down and the Logos took refuge in Vigo, Spain, to repair damages.

In December 1977 the *Logos* ceased to be *the* OM ship and became *one* of the OM ships. An older and larger ship was bought from the Costa Line in Italy and christened *Doulos*. This, too, brought a time of difficulty to the *Logos*. Many of her best people were sent to man the new acquisition and develop her ministry. With these experienced people on board, the *Doulos* set out for South America while the *Logos* continued her travels around Asia with many new and less experienced staff.

There had always been a problem on the *Logos* that with 140 people on board, those who were single or with shyer personalities tended to feel lost in the crowd. With so many new faces around at this time, this situation intensified, and the director, David Hicks, decided that what was needed was a strong small group structure on board. Everyone on the ship was assigned to a small group called a ship family. A married couple in each group functioned as 'parents' for the family. Each family was a random mixture of race, culture and sex. The object was to do things together as a normal family would. Sometimes this meant getting together in a cabin for prayer or for a relaxing time of coffee and conversation. Other times the 'family' would go ashore for an outing. Birthdays and other special days were always welcomed as times of festivity for the family.

By July, 1978, *Logos* was in Keelung, Taiwan. On the 26th, Adrian Kirk would be nine years old. Asked how he would like his ship family to celebrate the day, he replied, 'With a beach party.'

That sounded like a good idea. Enquiries were made about beaches in the area and a local man volunteered to take the group to one nearby. Two of the ship family were on duty and unable to go, but all the rest assembled in high spirits looking forward to the afternoon. At 2.00 p.m. they set out on the outing—an outing which was to end in tragedy.

Instead of the expanse of white sand they had been imagining, the beach turned out to be a rocky place. Further down the beach, though, the group could see fascinating rock formations carved out by wind and waves. That was the place to go for their picnic, they decided. The way was rough, leading through waist-deep water. Three of the men went on ahead with the bags while the others stayed back to help the children and women through the water. When the first three men arrived at the picnic spot, they carefully deposited the bags, changed into their swimming things and headed toward one of the many big rocks at the edge of the water. Catching sight of them, the local man who had volunteered his services as guide began shouting wildly to them in Mandarin—a language none of the three understood. The nightmare had begun.

One of the *Logos* men who had remained behind to help the women and children did understand Mandarin, and quickly explained that it was not safe where the three men were. They should come back immediately. The group began to shout and wave frantically, trying to get the attention of the men and communicate the urgent message to return. By this time Herbert Wagner was already in the water, but David Greenlee and Abel Ventura Castro turned to come back. Just as they did, a huge wave swept Abel off the rock.

Assuming Abel had been swept inland and was in no danger, Tony Kirk, the family 'father', made his way to the scene casually. What he found there shocked him deeply. Between two large rocks there was a deep gully. Herbert and Abel had both been swept into this gully and were obviously in serious trouble.

Tony looked around hastily for something he could use to help them and caught sight of a short bamboo pole. Not much, but by crouching down on the rock and stretching out as far as he could, Tony could just barely extend the pole far enough for Herbert to be able to reach it and draw himself to shore. As he pulled himself out of the water, the pole was jerked out of Tony's hand and was lost. Herbert, however, was safe.

Abel was on the opposite side of the gully. As the group shouted to him to swim back, he made no effort to respond. Within minutes the current swept him out of the gully and beyond reach. Frantically the group shouted to him and gestured wildly for him to swim to the left where there was a better chance of getting out. No response. A second, larger bamboo pole was found and thrown to him for support. Still no reaction from Abel, even though one of the men shouted in Spanish, Abel's native tongue. His face expressed no panic whatever. Just a peaceful, somewhat puzzled look. He didn't thrash or shout or wave; he just remained calm in the water. (Later the group surmised that he had been concussed by his fall from the rock.) The waves were big and each one covered him for increasingly longer periods of time until he lost consciousness and lay face down on the water.

Farther down the coast a couple of local young men had seen him and jumped into the water to try to rescue him. They were very strong swimmers who knew the waters and were able to reach him. But when they tried to bring him on shore, the waves caught them and threw them against the rocks, cutting them badly. Abel slipped away.

Fifteen minutes later he was recovered from the water at a much shallower place further down the coast. By this time he had been in the water more than thirty minutes. All attempts at resuscitation proved in vain. Abel had gone to be with the God he loved.

Ann Kirk, Tony's wife, tried to shield her children from the sight of death, but that was impossible. Tony arranged for a taxi to take the women and children back to the ship, where they instinctively huddled together in the Kirks' cabin; numb, shocked, reliving over and over in their minds the events of the afternoon.

It was Adrian and his sister Helen who finally pulled the women out of their numb state. 'Why are you all so sad?' they asked. 'Abel has gone to be with Jesus. That's the best place to be.'

How true, thought Ann. We have come to Taiwan to share the hope we have and here we sit huddled together in despair, shock and disbelief.

The party went on, but it was a quiet party, a time of praising God for Abel who had been willing to leave his home and family in Mexico to share with others what was most important to him.

For David Greenlee, who was right beside Abel when the accident occurred, the trauma was especially painful. Talking and praying with some of the others on the ship helped immensely to release some of the pent-up feelings. But when he had to write up reports for the police and when he had to be involved in much of the Spanish translation, the whole emotion-packed event was dragged through his mind again. David would often cry out to God in pain, saying, 'Lord, help me to go on.'

On Sunday evening as he was sitting in a church meeting listening to the speaker, he sensed the Lord speaking to him. 'David, Abel is alive. He's happy now. Are you going to rest in that and let me take your pain from you?'

David gave it all over to God, saying, 'I can't take it. You can have it, Lord.'

And God gave him peace.

13

The boat people

Clearly visible in the dim light of the overcast sky above the South China Sea was a small boat crowded with people, bobbing up and down on the waves. As the *Logos* drew nearer, people on board could see some of the fifty-three refugees, including seven children, crammed into the small fishing boat about twenty-five feet long.

Two years earlier, in 1978, when the *Logos* had sailed this same course on her way from Hong Kong to Thailand, there had been much discussion about what should be done if she were to encounter some of the 'boat people', Vietnamese families who risked their lives by fleeing their country in small, often unseaworthy fishing boats. In the event none had been sighted and the discussion had remained hypothetical. Now, on 3 October 1980, the situation was a reality that must be faced.

Many people felt that the answer was obvious; people in need must be taken on board and helped. In fact, the leaders of the *Logos* had been strongly warned against this course of action. 'Boat people' were not all genuine—some were pirates hoping to trap the unwary, and even genuine refugees might carry dangerous diseases that could affect the whole ship.

More serious was the problem of what to do with them

once they had been picked up. Many countries did not want to accept them and would refuse to allow them off the ship. Sometimes they would even refuse to allow a ship carrying refugees to enter the port. Thailand, where the *Logos* was headed, was already inundated with Vietnamese refugees and had a very strict attitude towards 'boat people'.

So the ship's leaders had decided to do what many refugee organisations advised—to provide the refugees with food, water, fuel, medicines and maps, and then leave the fishing boat to proceed on its way. An inflatable raft containing supplies was sent out to the refugees, and the situation was explained to their captain, who seemed to understand. But many of the *Logos* people found it impossible to accept. Even Des Harper, who as acting ship's director was responsible for the decision, wrote later:

> 'I really had some questions as to whether we were doing the right thing. Certainly we were doing what had been decided. But was it the right thing to do before the Lord? Here were people in a small boat, and even though we were giving them provisions to continue their journey to shore, everybody knew fairly well that their chances of making it in this little boat were very slim.'

Eventually, after much discussion and prayer, the leaders agreed that the refugees should be taken on board and their boat taken in tow. Near Thailand but still in international waters they would be returned to their boat to continue alone. In their own boat they would have a better chance of being accepted in Thailand. When the refugees came aboard the *Logos*, they would be put into quarantine on one of the decks until the doctor had time to examine them.

All of this took time. The ship's company was called together to be informed of the decision. When it was announced that the refugees would be taken aboard, everyone spontaneously and enthusiastically broke into applause. Tears were streaming down many faces.

The refugees, who proved to be ethnic Chinese, were helped on board, and each put through the welcoming rites.

First the long hair was cut. Then an anti-lice solution was put on the hair. Next came the stripping down, followed by a rigorous and thorough bath. Bags of clean used clothing were brought up from the holds where they had been stored. Fearing that the filth-encrusted clothing of the refugees might harbour disease, the *Logos* workers began to throw it overboard, replacing it with clothing from the bags. The refugees had meekly submitted to the whole procedure until it came to this point. But as they became aware that their old clothing was going to be thrown overboard, they began to protest vehemently. Taken aback, the *Logos* workers turned to the Chinese translators, trying to find out why the refugees were so upset. Gradually they realised that many of the refugees had sewed into the lining of their clothes what little money or other treasure they were able to bring with them. No wonder they were upset to see these clothes going into the sea!

A hasty discussion brought a solution acceptable to all. The filthy clothes were put into the little boat, which was being towed behind the ship. The refugees happily donned their new clothes. At least, some of them did. The women, accustomed to the long trousers of the traditional Vietnamese dress, found the skirts they were offered very strange. Eventually, however, everyone was outfitted in something acceptable.

Clean and freshly attired, they were taken one by one to a temporary clinic set up on the poop deck. There they were examined by the ship's doctor and questioned for names and a bit of basic information. The captain was there as well, along with Stella Chan, a Chinese nurse who served as translator.

The next step was met with obvious enjoyment. Food was set before them. No one had to explain what that meant!

By the time all the refugees had been processed and fed, it was well after supper-time. The ship's people were finished with the dining-room for the day, so it was cleared to make a place for the refugees to sleep on the floor. Someone from the book exhibition went down into the holds where books were stored and brought up a box of Vietnamese New Testaments which had been brought from Hong Kong. These were given to the refugees. The day ended with the Vietnamese stretched out comfortably on blankets on the floor, clean, freshly dressed, glowing with satisfaction in the aftermath of a good meal, many of them reading God's word for the first time. The *Logos* men and women, looking at the sight, again felt that familiar ache in their throats, as they swallowed to keep back tears.

Two mornings later another small boat was sighted about fifty or sixty miles off the coast of Vietnam. Naturally, everyone on the *Logos* immediately concluded that this must also be full of refugees. The boat, however, showed no sign of distress and made no attempt to attract attention. Not sure what to do, Captain Collins took the *Logos* in closer to investigate. The boat was somewhat larger than the one previously encountered by the *Logos*, and as she drew nearer, her company could see many people cowering under a tarpaulin as if in deadly fear of the approaching ship. The refugees on the *Logos*, instantly sympathetic to the plight of others, called out in Vietnamese, but they were too far away to be understood. The sight of a ship filled with shouting people bearing down upon them filled the occupants of the little boat with panic. Deathly afraid, they frantically tried to get their motor started. Black smoke poured out, but the motor refused to take hold.

Eventually they were able to catch the words of the captain of the first Vietnamese boat as he shouted to them and they were able to make out the Singaporean registration of the ship. The change was dramatic. A little white flag immediately went up to serve as a distress signal. Human figures emerged from under the tarpaulin and began waving their arms and shouting excitedly.

Quite obvious was the fact that there were some sick people in the boat. Also obvious was the fact that the boat was taking in water. Already there was some corrosion in the engine.

The decision to take these refugees aboard was reached much more quickly. Whereas the first boat had been filled mainly with ethnic Chinese, this one contained Vietnamese—forty of them. Several of them had served as officers in the South Vietnamese army. One of them, formerly chief of police in South Vietnam, had suffered a couple of strokes while in concentration camp and was very weak; he had to be lifted by stretcher on to the *Logos*.

These boat people had apparently been without food and water for a day or two. Though several appeared quite ill, the doctor found no serious disease. The problem seemed to be largely severe seasickness and exhaustion. Two or three needed to have intravenous fluids for a couple of days.

This brought the number of refugees on board to ninety-three, ranging in age from three months to seventy-nine years. Logos was already filled to her capacity of 142. The remaining two days of the voyage to Thailand would have to be endured under extremely cramped conditions.

Then came a new development which overturned the carefully-laid plans. The larger fishing boat in tow began filling with water and collided forcefully with the other boat. Its mooring rope broke and the boat sank rapidly. Sometime during the night the second boat disappeared as well. The *Logos* was left with no choice but to try to sail into Thailand with all the refugees aboard.

Meanwhile, in Thailand, the line-up men, Lloyd Nicholas and Chan Thye Huat, had been strongly warned by the chief of immigration that the ship should not pick up any Vietnamese boat people because that would cause immense problems. The Thai government did not classify the boat people as refugees because they did not recognise the war in Vietnam. They were considered as illegal immigrants and treated in some cases as spies.

With some degree of apprehension the *Logos* company wondered what would happen when the ship reached Songkhla, her first port in Thailand. Would she be able to disembark their passengers? Would the crew and staff be able to carry out their programme? Would the ship even be allowed to come into port?

To their amazement, when they reached Songkhla, they were immediately allowed to dock, even though the authorities knew that the refugees were aboard. The refugees themselves were strictly confined to the ship; they could not even put one foot on the quayside. With this one restriction the *Logos* was given complete freedom to continue on with her book exhibition and programme as if the refugees were not even there.

Some Swedish missionaries who had been given money specifically for refugee work felt that God wanted them to use the money to provide food for the *Logos* refugees for as long as they were in Songkhla. A local restaurant owner brought steaming pots of the most delicious-smelling food to set before the refugees—morning, noon and night. Lloyd Nicholas went to Bangkok to talk with the acting British consul, who proved to be very friendly and sympathetic to the situation of the *Logos*.

'Don't worry,' he assured Lloyd, 'it should take only three or four days to clear up the matter. There have been a couple of similar cases in the past few weeks. They were cleared up easily.'

He then explained that the usual procedure was that a foreign government must guarantee to resettle the refugees within thirty days. During these thirty days the UNHCR (United Nations High Commission for Refugees) would take responsibility for the people, and they would be allowed to disembark.

But a week later the British consul called Lloyd to his office to inform him that the British government did not consider it their responsibility to resettle the refugees. According to international agreement, if the country of the first port of entry (Thailand) did not accept them, then the government of the country where the ship was registered (Singapore) was next in line. But Singapore, already facing the problem of an overpopulated country, had been consistently refusing to accept any refugees. However, rather than give an immediate clear answer in this case, they stalled. As long as there was no clear refusal, no other country would consider the problem. When finally Singapore did issue a pointblank refusal, Britain, next in line because the company owning *Logos* was British, decided to try to force Singapore to reconsider.

Under great pressure to resolve the situation quickly, the ship headquarters in Germany started looking for contact to highly-placed officials in various governments or organisations who might use their influence to help. High-level negotiations were carried on with the Home and Foreign Offices in London.

Prayer supporters of OM around the world were alerted and an incredible amount of prayer took place. Again the ship ministry was in a situation in which it desperately needed the intervention of God. Government negotiations could drag on for months without accomplishing anything. But God could do the seemingly impossible.

For the refugees this time of waiting was especially hard. Ninety-three people were packed into the small area of the poop deck, sitting or lying around idly on blankets stretched out on the deck, waiting for time to pass. As the poop deck was normally the play area for the ship children, the ship children were deprived of a place to play. But their mothers took them to the poop deck anyway and went around chatting with the various refugees. Other ship people, too, as they had free time, would wander back to chat. For some of the refugees who had shown a deep spiritual hunger, Bible classes were started. English classes, too, were set up to help prepare the refugees for their new lives.

All this, however, occupied only a fraction of the many hours in a day. The refugees needed and wanted more activity. Soon they were scattered around the ship helping out in many different areas. Among them was a family of skilled welders who proved of great help. An engineer found his way down to the engine room. Other refugees scraped paint, washed dishes, folded clothes in the laundry room; in short, they integrated beautifully into ship life. They were given little tags to wear that read 'Special Guest' and visitors who met them never even guessed that they were refugees.

October was the time of the year when the major *Logos* personnel changes occurred. Many workers who had been on the ship for one or two years left to go home, to be replaced by fifty-three new recruits in Bangkok. Some had to leave a bit early, going from Songkhla and leaving gaps in the work force, gaps that were filled by the Vietnamese. When the new workers arrived in Bangkok, some of them were trained into their new jobs by Vietnamese refugees!

The boat people, who at first had been objects of compassion, soon became warmly-appreciated friends. With delight the nurses watched the three-month-old baby, once limp like a rag doll, grow strong and fat and healthy as his mother's dried-up breasts swelled with a supply of nourishing milk. Kathy Dillner, one of the nurses, talked about an experience with the stroke victim, a man of fifty-seven who looked as if he were seventy. Though he was aware of everything going on around him, he could neither move significantly nor talk.

'I had quite a bit to do with this old man. Quite frequently I had to put drops in his eyes. As I did things for him, I would talk to him in English and I knew he understood me because he'd nod to show he knew what I was talking about, even though he couldn't answer me. So I talked to him about the Lord and why we loved the boat people and why we loved him.

'One day his daughter came to me and said excitedly, "My father just spoke. It's the first time I've heard him speak since we came out of prison camp."

' "What did he say?" I wanted to know.

' "He said, 'I want to be a Christian.' "

'I went and got a couple of the Chinese brothers to pray with him. As we prayed, tears were just pouring down his cheeks. He might not have any of the things you and I have—no worldly goods—but that man has found eternal life!'

The doctor had to leave the ship as soon as it docked in Songkhla because he had to get back to his clinic in the northern part of Thailand. The two nurses were left with the awesome responsibility of caring not only for the ship crew and staff but also for the refugees who were confined to the ship. In case of emergency they knew they could get in touch with the doctor at a nearby refugee camp, but that was still quite a distance.

About 5.00 a.m. on the morning after the doctor left, Kathy was awakened by a banging on her door.

'Oh no,' she groaned to her husband, 'I don't want to answer it. What's it going to be?'

Her fears were realised as she opened her cabin door and saw a Vietnamese mother holding her sobbing child. The little boy had jammed his finger in a steel door and it was just dangling. Kathy took him to the ship's clinic while she sent her husband off to the refugees' camp for a doctor. It seemed to take forever for the doctor to arrive, When he did, there was nothing he could do to save the finger.

Some time later, when the ship was sailing the short distance from Songkhla to Bangkok, the *Logos* family had organised a 'fun' night for the refugees, a talent night at which the *Logos* men and women sang silly songs, did funny skits and dances—anything they could think of to make their guests laugh. Right in the front row sat this little boy with a big bandage on his finger and an expression of pure joy on his face.

As the political wrangling about resettling the refugees dragged on, the *Logos* had to cancel her next port of call and remain in Thailand. Finally the Port Authority issued an ultimatum. The *Logos* had already overstayed the time for which she had permission. In one week she would have to leave, regardless of whether the refugee problem was settled or not. More pressure was put on the British government. Finally, on 22 November the British government agreed to accept responsibility for the refugees and guarantee their resettlement. On 27 November, the last day of the week of grace and Thanksgiving Day to the Americans on board, the refugees were able to walk down the gangway in Bangkok and be taken to the resettlement camp where they would remain until the UNHCR was able to get them resettled in various countries. Most of them would go to Britain. They had been almost eight weeks on the ship.

It was a hard moment for the refugees and for those staying on board. Emotions were mixed. Many of the refugees had turned to Jesus Christ while on the ship. Most of the others made a similar decision in the resettlement camp, where they had contact with Christians. In the years that followed, their stories trickled back, describing difficulties in adjusting to new cultures and circumstances, but also of joys and encouragement found in knowing God and being able to turn to him for help.

Nearly eight years later, Graham Wells, the last director of the *Logos*, encountered one of these refugees under rather unusual circumstances. While Graham was setting up his office as the *Logos* representative in Birmingham, England, he learned that a group of Chinese Christians met in part of the same building for church services. One day Graham got into conversation with one of the leaders of the church.

'You were on the *Logos*?' exclaimed the Chinese Christian in astonishment when Graham began to explain who he was and what he was doing. 'The *Logos* saved my life. I was in a small fishing boat off the coast of Vietnam . . .'

14

A dream come true

The idea of bringing the ship to Communist China had first surfaced in about 1978, when some of her people had the opportunity to visit China. At that time it had seemed a dream, a beautiful but wildly improbable idea. A Christian ship like the *Logos* would never be able to get permission to enter China. But the idea refused to die. Workers in OM had been praying for China for years. Somehow, sometime, they were confident, God was going to do something great in that country. Perhaps in some small way he might use the *Logos*. Certainly it was worth investigating the possibilities.

In early 1980 the Logos was in the general area of China. Furthermore, later in the year she had a small block of time which had not yet been scheduled. Perhaps, just perhaps, there might be a possibility of going to China then. A far-fetched idea, but one that deserved to be considered at least. Two men from the *Logos* were sent; Peter Conlan, an Englishman, and Go Teg Chin, a Chinese from the Philippines. Teg Chin was able to get a visa fairly easily but the only way Peter could get one was to join a tour group. He chose a tour that would spend four days in Beijing (Peking), the capital of China.

The tour proved to be a memorable experience for

Peter. With fascination he observed the contrasts of that great country, often totally unprepared for what he saw: Canton, with its huge billboards advertising Johnny Walker whisky, American Express credit cards and Canon cameras; the clean comfortable express train with its contributions toward gracious living—a ridiculously cheap cup of tea served by embarrassingly attentive waiters, a colour television presenting well-produced films of Chinese industrial development or depicting China's extraordinary prowess in gymnastics. (Peter was particularly amused by one extraordinary gentleman who was bending metal bars around his throat!)

Then there was the countryside deep within China, the 'people's landscape', vast and bleak. Its cities were drab, grey, austere, its inhabitants caught up in the harsh reality of life.

It was the people who most impressed Peter. Everywhere he went he was met with helpfulness and delightful openness from warmhearted, hospitable, friendly men and women. Many times young people would stop him on the street, eager for an opportunity to practise their English.

Most precious of all Peter's memories were those of the hours he and Teg Chin were able to slip away from the tour group, make their way furtively through the back streets of a city and slip secretly into the home of Chinese Christians. What a privilege he considered it to be able to receive the simple but generously shared hospitality of these believers in their tiny, cold, primitively-furnished apartments and to hear their inspiring testimonies of God's faithfulness to them in the midst of the crushing weight of the sufferings they had gone through.

Another deeply-implanted memory was the visit to a building where they watched printing presses clattering away as they turned out Communist booklets with monotonous regularity. The building had once been a church. During the Cultural Revolution red guards had stormed in and ransacked the building, destroying all its Christian contents. The rubble was carted out. Printing presses were moved in. The place of worship was converted into a factory producing atheistic propaganda.

This was the China of 1980. The tour proved an eye-opening experience. The attempt to contact government officials and lay the groundwork for a *Logos* visit, however, proved discouraging. Peter and Teg Chin were able to talk with some officials, but the talks were characterised by a marked lack of enthusiasm. Peter and Teg Chin managed to find out that the best avenue of entry would probably be through the Ministry of Book Import and Export. And they did manage to get the ministry of Overseas Chinese Affairs to agree to send an invitation for them to return to China to talk business.

After further visits to Beijing by Teg Chin, an invitation was issued to both Teg Chin and Peter to return for final discussions. Negotiations with the three departments co-ordinating book imports, shipping and tourism resulted in a signed invitation for the ship to visit. With this in hand, Peter and Teg Chin flew 700 miles south to Shanghai to make arrangements for the docking of the ship. Word had evidently gone before them, for they now were treated with the greatest deference, with the negotiations culminating in a ten-course gourmet meal at an exclusive government restaurant.

Before leaving Shanghai, Peter and Teg Chin slipped unobtrusively through the dark back streets to emerge quietly at the door of Christian friends. With obvious delight on their faces, the elderly couple listened attentively to the report of the ship's coming. More than 300 house fellowships of Christians meeting all over Shanghai had been and would be praying for this visit, Peter and Teg Chin were assured.

This visit to China, the *Logos* people realised, would be something quite different from their usual visits to a port. As a matter of fact, hemmed in by so many restrictions, there seemed little that the ship could actually do. No one would be allowed to visit the ship, though the ship personnel themselves would be able to come and go freely in the city. No book exhibition could take place on the ship. However, one could be held in Beijing. The government would provide the hall and the transport of books from the ship to Beijing. The exhibition would differ in several ways from the usual one: it would be overwhelmingly educational, though about thirty Christian titles would be slipped in among the several hundred general ones, and the books could not be sold. People could come in and look at them as much as they liked, but they could not buy. For all practical purposes, the book exhibition would function as a library rather than as a bookshop.

Ship personnel would be allowed to visit churches but they could not speak publicly in any services. They could talk freely with people they met on the street, as long as they did it discreetly so as not to attract a crowd. No Christian books could be taken off the ship unless they were also returned to the ship, so there was no possibility of getting much-craved-for Bibles into the hands of local Christians. And finally, almost all the ship people must participate in a five-day tour at some point during the visit.

In spite of these suffocating restrictions, men and women on the *Logos* were able to see the hand of God at work in many small ways. When the ship came into Shanghai, swarms of customs officials came aboard. They wandered everywhere, asking questions, taking pictures, enquiring into the work of the ship's company. Throughout the ship's stay in Shanghai there were always some of these officials on board to make sure that nothing out of order was done by the ship people. Far from being obnoxious, these men were openly curious and increasingly friendly. They were bewildered but impressed by this example of communal living at its best; men and women living and working closely together in obvious harmony—

living simply, and yet happily. They knew many who had these ideals but few who achieved them. What was the secret of these young people? Often these officials could be found listening in at ship devotions or sitting in the ship library reading books—Christian books—or listening to taped messages from Christian leaders. One evening Allan Adams, the ship director, had to go ashore on business.

'Oh no,' the official at the gangway told him in mock seriousness, 'you can't go off now. Tonight is the night when the ship people pray.' He was referring to the customary evening of prayer held on the ship every week.

On the first day in Shanghai ten government officials flew down from Beijing and, joined by forty more from Shanghai, attended a reception on the *Logos*. The purpose of the reception was to build relationships with these people and to help them understand a bit more what this strange ship was all about. Slides of the ship's ministry in other ports were accompanied by a commentary to explain them. Music by the ship's choir provided entertainment. Finally, Allan Adams gave a short speech in which he referred to the community life on the ship and emphasised the desire of the ship's personnel to learn through this visit to China. At the time he also stated clearly that the men and women on the ship were committed to following the teachings of the Bible, or at least, trying to do so. After the reception the officials were offered a tour of the ship, including the book exhibition as it would normally be set up in other countries. No books, of course, were offered for sale this time.

In Beijing each day between 700 and 1,000 people visited the book exhibition, which was held in the National Art Gallery. By surrendering his identity card, each person obtained the right to borrow a book and read it at one of the many tables provided. People could be seen all over the hall sitting at tables, their heads bent over a book, deeply absorbed in its contents. Frequently they could be seen taking notes, sometimes even copying whole pages. Obviously they were a people thirsty for knowledge. Not just the educational books disappeared from the shelves; Christian books proved popular as well. Logos workers noted with interest that IVP's *New Illustrated Bible Dictionary* and Walter Trobisch's *I Married You* seemed to be among the most popular Christian books.

An attractive blue-and-white leaflet with a picture of the *Logos* and her crew and staff was printed for the *Logos* people to use. The text inside, written in both Chinese and English, read

'MV *Logos*—THE WISDOM SHIP

'The "Wisdom Ship", now visiting China, is a floating Educational Book Exhibition which in the past ten years has visited 230 ports in 68 different countries of the world. Over three million people have visited the ship. The crew and staff of the ship come from over twenty-five different countries. All are Christians serving as volunteers and do not receive any salary. Easterners and Westerners live, learn and work together as one community. They are sometimes called a "Floating United Nations". Their objective is to serve the peoples of Asia by bringing literature that will enlighten minds and help people everywhere to understand the true meaning of life.

'We are delighted to be able to visit China and wish to make friends with the Chinese people and learn more about this great country. Because we ourselves have experienced the love of God revealed in our Lord Jesus Christ, we give you the Christian greeting: "Peace be unto you." '

The term 'Wisdom Ship' was taken from a report on the *Logos* that was published in a magazine of the Book Import and Export Department in Beijing—an honest and favourable report, incidentally.

As *Logos* men and women went ashore and encountered people in the parks, on the streets, or anywhere else, they were able to give them this leaflet and use this as a starting point for conversation. Often these conversations developed into opportunities to talk about God, with the Chinese listening attentively as *Logos* workers shared what they had experienced personally.

The *Logos* people had hoped to be able to distribute Chinese Bibles ashore. With this in mind they had laid in a good supply. The restriction prohibiting this was a huge disappointment. The restriction was rigidly enforced. Each time people left the ship, their passport numbers were written down and they were checked to see what they might be carrying ashore. One Bible each could be carried, but the fact was duly noted down and on their return they must be able to show that they were bringing them back. No big thing was made of this, but workers on the *Logos* nevertheless felt they were getting a tiny— very, very tiny—taste of what life must be like for Christians in China.

Accustomed to being the ones who ministered in the church services they attended, the *Logos* family found themselves on the receiving end of the blessing in China. To their amazement they found some of the churches packed, with people crowding into the aisles and spilling out into the courtyards. Yet, sadly, young people were conspicuous by their absence. Nevertheless, it was both humbling and inspiring to look into the faces of these older Christians and to try to imagine the horrible suffering that many of them had undoubtedly experienced, suffering that only served to draw them closer to God.

At the time of the *Logos* visit, the church in China was basically split into two groups. The open church was supported by the government, its pastors placed by the government, and its compliance with government directives obvious, at least on the visible level. Then there were the house-fellowship meetings held secretly in private homes, with believers who were determined to be free to worship as their conscience dictated without government influence or control. Both groups contained godly, dedicated believers, though one tended to be critical of the other. *Logos* was accepted freely by both groups, enabling her people to get a glimpse into both aspects of the Chinese church and experience the warm fellowship of a wide variety of Christians. Many of the *Logos* crew and staff, too, were invited to visit the homes of Christians from both kinds of churches.

David Adeney, a missionary in China for many years before the Communist takeover, was able to sail on the *Logos* as she entered China, helping the *Logos* people to understand the country better and to analyse more accurately what they saw and heard. Of one of the open churches he visited, Mr Adeney wrote:

'In Hangchow, long before the service started, the church was completely filled, including the courtyard. People were sitting everywhere, even on the stairs to the gallery and the whole place was crowded with about a thousand people . . . . When the leader of the service led in prayer, there was a very warm response as most of the congregation added their "Amens". The message was given on the story of Mary and Martha and emphasised dedication to the service of the Lord and his Church . . . . There was no doubt about the spiritual fervour of many who attended the service. On a previous Friday evening, three of us had visited the choir practice and had a talk with one of the old pastors. He told us that 300 had been baptised last year and another 200 this year. He said that because the church was so crowded, with about 3,000 people attending the three services on Sunday, the Government had agreed to help in obtaining the opening of another and larger church building.'

Appalled at the amount of money that must be spent for the compulsory tours, the *Logos* men and women were nevertheless thrilled with the prospect of getting to see more of this intriguing country. The five-day tour into inland China was crowded with rapidly-changing impressions, giving the sightseers perhaps a superficial view of China yet helping immensely in getting a mental overall picture, a framework on which to hang the details of real encounters with people. Wherever they went, they found people friendly and ready to talk. Many knew some English, confiding that they had studied it in school or on their own at night.

At the end of the visit Chinese officials gave a farewell banquet for officers and leaders on the ship and expressed the hope that the *Logos* would come to China again.

As the ship sailed away from Shanghai, the *Logos* family, used to much more visible and active evangelism, asked themselves if the visit had been worth the time, energy and money it cost. Certainly it had been an unforgettable experience, but had it really accomplished anything?

'Yes,' the veteran missionary David Adeney assured them emphatically.

In the first place, he said, the visit of the *Logos* had stimulated an immense amount of prayer for China. *Logos* people themselves had gained first-hand experience of the situation in China, which should motivate them to pray more fervently and be able to do so more intelligently, and by passing on information to other people, stimulate them also in prayer.

Then, the very presence of the ship was in itself a witness. Lying there in the harbour of Shanghai, clearly visible to everyone and widely known to be a Christian ship—this very fact communicated something to the Chinese people. The book exhibition in Beijing with its Christian books, few in number but clearly displayed, spoke its message as well. Two years earlier a public display of the Bible would never have been allowed. Its very presence there on the shelves in the National Art Gallery proclaimed the fact that Christianity was no longer illegal.

'Never underestimate either,' continued Mr Adeney, 'the importance of all contacts with individual people which were made. Seed was sown; what fruit it brings forth is in God's hands.

'Also realise that the Christians in China have been isolated for nearly thirty years. Any sense of there being a large body of Christians outside of China, loving them, supporting them, concerned for them, brings encouragement. I believe that the visit of the ship to China at this time did bring encouragement to the Christians.

'And finally, the visit of the ship provided a realistic basis to seek God's will about future involvement with China in some way. Of course, at this moment we cannot determine what shape that involvement may take, but certainly the first link in a chain of future involvement has been forged.'

15

Doors close—doors open

Weeks before the *Logos* planned to visit a port, the line-up team would be sent ahead to make arrangements and to obtain all official permissions for entry, embarkation, book-selling, and whatever else was necessary in order to carry out the programme. This involved an immense amount of work and frustration, but in the end the permissions were nearly always obtained. Nearly always.

Once, in 1973, *Logos* was refused permission to enter Indonesia, and no amount of prayer or persuasion was able to change that decision. God, it seemed had his reasons for not making the visit possible, and the *Logos* people had to trust in him. The next year, in 1974, *Logos* was refused permission to go to Sri Lanka, but after much prayer and a personal appeal by Sri Lankan Christians to the Prime Minister, the decision was reversed.

As the *Logos* sailed into Alexandria, Egypt, in August of 1982, however, her people were not worried about permissions. Months of painstaking labour by the line-up team had resulted in the obtaining of all permissions in writing. So, as the ship docked at a central berth, her people looked forward with happy anticipation to a full programme in port. But that programme never took place.

Two hours after the ship tied up, a series of puzzling incidents took place. Permission had been given for local people to enter the port area to visit the ship; that permission was cancelled. Landing cards had been issued to the *Logos* company so the crew and staff could go ashore; these were confiscated. Several security police took up positions on board and on the quayside beside the ship. To enquiries of the bewildered ship people, the officials had only one answer, 'We have our orders.'

A short time later the ship was ordered to move to a nearby anchorage. But people could still go out to the ship in small launches to carry on business. Then the ship was ordered to move further out to a remote anchorage about ten miles outside the port area, beyond the reach of the launch service. The port control office and the *Logos* shipping agent were instructed to avoid all radio communication with the ship, so calls over the ship radio were ignored. The ship was completely isolated, stuck at anchor and cut off from all contact with the outside world.

The ship family, understandably shaken up by the experience, did the only thing they could do. They turned to God. Leaders on the ship called them together for a day of prayer and fasting. Sensing a further need for prayer, the men and women themselves extended it on into the next days. A prayer chain was started so that at any hour of the day or night someone was praying. At first the theme of the prayers was to get back into Alexandria, but slowly the focus changed. Egypt itself became the target. The people prayed that God would work in a mighty way in Egypt. Finally, as Frank Fortunato, who was acting ship's director at the time, described it:

'God then began to show us that, more important than our ministry in the port, were the lives of those who were representing him. We began to pray for revival. People started getting their lives right with God. Husbands and wives began to get things right in their relationship. This led to open times of confession, and then to exhilarating worship and celebration. We were experiencing revival on board with all the buoyancy and excitement of meeting with God . . . '

Meanwhile, back in Alexandria the line-up team worked feverishly to try to break the impasse. Hours of running around from one office to another, and numerous attempts to contact high officials proved fruitless. Eventually the security police reluctantly offered an explanation. A powerful anti-*Logos* lobby had developed because of the strong Christian emphasis of the 1976 visit of *Logos*, said the police. Especially fanatical in their hatred of the ship was the militantly religious Islamic Brotherhood in Alexandria. Bomb threats had been made. What the officials had done to the *Logos*, they explained, was for the ship's own safety.

From local Christians the line-up team learned that there had been incidents of violence directed toward Christians and Christian property in recent weeks. Bombs had injured worshippers and damaged property at some churches, so armed guards had been posted at all church meetings, courtesy of the government.

Finally, after five days, the ship was allowed to communicate with the line-up workers ashore and with the ship's headquarters in Germany. Allan Adams, the ship's director, was in Germany because his wife had just given birth to a child. He had been kept fully informed of the situation, and had discussed the matter with leaders at the ship's headquarters. Allan told Frank Fortunato that Christians in Lebanon had invited the *Logos* to visit their country.

At that point Frank exploded. The Israelis had invaded Lebanon! The country was at war! Every day news reports vividly described the havoc wrought by bombing and shelling of West Beirut. Under no circumstances, shouted Frank, would he allow the ship to go to Lebanon! Didn't Allan remember that there were women and children aboard?

When Bertil, the OM co-ordinator for the Arab world, had first phoned the headquarters to say he had heard about the *Logos* situation, had prayed about it and believed that God wanted the ship to go to Lebanon, ship leaders were taken by surprise. Aware of the situation in Lebanon, they had never even considered it as a possibility. But some solution to the problem had to be found. The *Logos* had planned to spend two and a half weeks in Egypt. What could be done with those extra weeks?

A day or two later Bertil called again and said, 'I know you think I'm wandering in my mind, but I really feel that God wants the *Logos* to go to Lebanon.'

Just a few hours after this second phone call from Bertil, news came over radio and television that the Palestinian Liberation Organisation had agreed to pull out of Lebanon and the Israelis were making plans to evacuate them. That news made the leaders at headquarters stop and reconsider. Was God opening up the way? They decided that the only way they could find out was to send someone to Lebanon to assess the situation. Lloyd Nicholas, one of the most experienced line-up men, was sent from Germany the next day.

All of this was communicated to Frank on the *Logos*. Frank called together the *Logos* family and informed them. He felt keenly the weight of responsibility on him as he faced this momentous decision. The people on the ship were the ones who would be most affected by the decision; he wanted them to know the situation and to pray with him for guidance. In the meantime the *Logos* steamed on to Cyprus to pick up needed water and other supplies and to wait for news from Lebanon.

Lloyd Nicholas was unable to fly directly to Lebanon because of the security situation; he decided to go via Cyprus and obtain a visa there. The first morning after his arrival in Cyprus, Lloyd went to the Lebanese embassy in Larnaca and said he wanted to go to Lebanon and explained why.

'Sorry. We're not issuing visas to anyone at the time because, as you probably know, we're trying to evacuate the Palestinians from Lebanon.'

'Look,' said Lloyd, 'I really need to go to Lebanon. I'm representing a ship. We want to take the ship to your country.' And he went on to explain what the ship was all about. After excusing himself for a brief talk with the consul, the man returned to Lloyd, took his passport, and disappeared with it. About fifteen minutes later he came back with the visa stamped into the passport and signed. Lloyd stared at it in wonder. Was this confirmation of God's leading? Nowhere does a person get a visa in half an hour—at least not in his experience.

The only way to get into Lebanon was to take one of the ferries that were being used to evacuate the Palestinians. Late that same night Lloyd boarded one of these ferries. There was no lounge or cabin accommodation— just an open deck with deck chairs scattered around, which were occupied by newsmen, their camera crews and equipment. Before the ferry got to Lebanon, an Israeli gunboat checked out all the names on the crew and passenger list. Then the ferry was allowed to go on into port, arriving early in the afternoon.

Bertil had tried to get a message through to the Bible Society representative in Beirut. Lloyd could only hope that the message had got through and that the man would be at the pier to meet him. When he arrived, however, no one was there.

All Lloyd had was the name of the man and the name of the suburb in which he lived. No street address. In the end, he took a taxi to the suburb and found a nearby Bible college, where someone was able to tell him the address he wanted.

When Lloyd arrived at the house, the man he was looking for was not at home, but his niece assured Lloyd that he would be coming home soon. Lloyd was invited to sit down and make himself comfortable. Setting his bags down, he walked to the living-room to relax with a glass of cool orange juice. But just as he was about to sit down, the whole hillside erupted into a deafening roar— machine gun-fire, cannon blasts, and explosions. 'Oh no,' groaned Lloyd, 'why did I ever come here to Lebanon in the middle of a war? The peace was certainly shortlived. Who knows if I'll ever get out of this situation?'

Stunned, Lloyd just stood there, not knowing what to do. Obviously, the safest thing would be to take cover, but he turned toward the door instead. At that moment the niece rushed into the room, calling out, 'There's nothing to worry about. They're just celebrating the election of the new president.'

An hour later Lucien Accad, the man from the Bible Society, arrived with another Christian man. They were very excited about the prospect of the *Logos* coming to Lebanon. Lloyd had to explain that no decision had been reached yet, and asked whom they should approach to see whether the *Logos* would be able to come. This simple question caused some bafflement. The Lebanese government was clearly not relevant to this situation. Finally, Mr Accad's cousin was contacted for advice. He also was not sure whom to ask, but he thought that another cousin, who worked in the military, might be able to contact the man they needed.

Early in the morning the second 'cousin' came around to pick Lloyd up. Together they went down into West Beirut, wound through a labyrinth of narrow streets and ended up at a little sports-shoe shop.

'Are we meeting here?' asked Lloyd in surprise.

'Yes, of course. This is my family shoe shop. He feels safest coming here.'

This was not at all Lloyd's conception of what should happen. He had expected to go to some government building and meet someone behind a desk. But this kind of thing? Lloyd couldn't help feeling despondently that this was going to be a fruitless discussion, more time wasted going up a dead-end street.

Three minutes later two big men in Lebanese army uniform strode briskly into the store. One carried a walkie-talkie in his hand; the other, a machine gun. The one with the machine gun stood at the door while the one with the walkie-talkie went into a back room. The 'cousin' said to Lloyd, 'You go with him,' indicating the man with the walkie-talkie.

Inside the back room, the army officer turned to Lloyd and asked, 'What do you want?'

'Well, we want to bring the *Logos* here to Lebanon.'

For the next five minutes Lloyd explained what the *Logos* was and why he wanted to bring the ship to Lebanon. He talked about the book exhibition, but he also said that the *Logos* was a Christian ship and her people wanted to come to Lebanon to share the message of Jesus Christ. All this time the army man was silently looking down at an album of ship photographs that Lloyd had assembled to explain the ministry of the ship. When Lloyd came to the end of what he had to say, he asked hesitantly, 'What do you think?' Lifting his eyes from the album and looking straight into Lloyd's eyes, the army officer said, 'You are welcome in Lebanon.'

Confused by an answer like that, Lloyd stammered, 'Thank you very much. I appreciate that I'm welcome in Lebanon. But what about the *Logos*?'

'Yes,' the man repeated, 'you are welcome in Lebanon.'

'Do you mean that the *Logos* can come to Lebanon?'

'Yes, yes. Bring your ship. If you want it to come this afternoon, no problem. I'll make arrangements for you.'

'Well, don't I need to go and see anybody else?'

'No. Just bring your ship.'

Not knowing how to respond to that, Lloyd finally said uncertainly, 'Thank you very much.'

The army man turned and walked out. Lloyd never saw him again.

Still bemused, Lloyd picked up his photo book and returned to the front part of the shop, where the rest of the family had by this time gathered.

'What did he say?' asked the 'cousin' eagerly.

'He said, "You're welcome in Lebanon." '

At these words the 'cousin' got very excited and started jumping up and down, waving his arms and praising God.

'Does this really mean that the *Logos* can come to Lebanon?' asked Lloyd sceptically.

'We can go to the army headquarters and check, if you like.'

'Yes, let's do that just to make two hundred per cent sure.'

At the army headquarters they found a man with a lot of gold on his shoulders and told him, 'We met So-and-so and he said the *Logos* could come to Lebanon.'

'Yes, I've already heard about that. When is your ship coming? We want to make arrangements.'

'Wow,' thought Lloyd, 'word sure gets around fast here!' But at that point he realised that the *Logos* really could come to Lebanon. No written permission was necessary. 'You're welcome in Lebanon.' That one sentence spoken by one man in the back of a shoe shop was all that was needed.

Full of excitement, Lloyd now wanted to let the *Logos* know that the ship could come. That was more difficult than it sounds. The telecommunications center had been blown up. Telephones were not working. Telex machines were not working. There was no way to send a telegram. Almost bursting with eagerness to tell the *Logos* the exciting news and fighting frustration at the fact that there seemed to be no way to do it, Lloyd started looking for a Mr Roukoz, who worked in telecommunications. The search for this man took until after sunset. Finally Lloyd found the right house.

'Helio,' he said, 'I'm Lloyd Nicholas . . .'

'Oh, yes. I've been waiting for you all day. What's taken you so long?'

'I need to contact the *Logos* . . .' Lloyd began.

'Yes, I know. I have a little VHF radio set here in my house. Maybe we can get into contact that way. I'll try to contact a shipping agent in Cyprus and maybe he can put us in touch with the ship.'

Soon Mr Roukoz was in touch with the agent. After that, there was nothing to do but wait and see what the agent could do. Lloyd sat and talked with Mr Roukoz, enjoying some more good Lebanese hospitality as they waited impatiently. Half an hour later the agent called back. He was in touch with the *Logos*. In a few minutes Lloyd was talking with Frank Fortunato, who was standing on the bridge of the *Logos*. Lloyd could hear him as clearly as if he were in the same room. Eagerly Lloyd related the events of the day. Plans were made for the ship to come in two days.

Arrangements were made to get into contact again the following evening, same time, same place. But no matter how he tried, the next night Lloyd could not get through to the *Logos*. The normal range of the radio set was only twenty miles. Cyprus was 120 miles away! It was only because of unusually good atmospheric conditions and the elevated location of the house that Lloyd had been able to get through on the previous evening. If he'd come a few hours earlier or a few hours later, he might not have been able to get through. Lloyd knew, though, that it was not just coincidence. It was the hand of God at work to meet a particular need at a particular time.

Because the Palestinians were being evacuated from Beirut, it was not possible for the ship to go to Beirut. Instead, the *Logos* went to Jounieh, a small port six kilometres north of Beirut. The water was not deep enough at the pier for the *Logos*, so she had to anchor about 500 metres from shore. Visitors were transported to and from the ship at first by the *Logos* lifeboat and later by a launch.

People in Lebanon were tired of the war. The war just brought suffering and pain to them. There was no hope, no physical salvation for them. The message brought by the *Logos* did offer hope. Many, many people responded to it. Christians were amazed; they had never seen such openness before.

In the past, said one missionary, tract distribution had been forbidden; anyone who tried it was harassed and the tracts destroyed. But this time the message was eagerly received and read. At one busy intersection six *Logos* people were able to pass out over 5,000 tracts in one hour.

During the daytime men and women from the *Logos* went door-to-door selling Christian books and talking with people. Open-air meetings were held. An International Night, the *Logos* cultural show with a Christian message, gave three performances at the biggest shopping mall in the city. Several hundred people stood around and watched. At one point the speaker drew an illustration of the cross and explained what Jesus' death on the cross meant; the audience responded with a spontaneous outburst of applause.

Everywhere there were people who responded to the message and committed themselves to Christ. Many others went to the ship to talk further. One young lady who had watched the International Night came to the ship the following day. She had seen something in the faces of the performers, something she did not have but she wanted. She found it as she accepted Jesus' offer of forgiveness and new life.

The man in charge of the launch service had 'connections'. Within twenty-four hours he had arranged a VIP reception which drew more than ninety people, including such dignitaries as an ex-president of Lebanon, a brother-in-law of the new president, the patriarch of the Maronite Church, and many other government and religious leaders as well as a number of leading businessmen. Formally in speeches and testimonies and informally in private conversations the *Logos* men and women told the message of hope that they were bringing to Lebanon. At the end of the reception the former president gave an unplanned speech.

Hundreds of people visited the book exhibition in spite of the fact that they had to go by launch. As the ship began making preparations to sail at six o'clock of the last day, people were still trying to get to the ship to buy books, even hiring private launches to take them. Along with the educational books, many, many Christian books were sold, including Bibles and commentaries purchased by several bishops and priests of the dominant Maronite Catholic Church.

The *Logos* left Lebanon on 30 August. A week later the new president was assassinated and the country was plunged into fierce fighting again, turmoil that would drag on and on. Those few days were the only days of relative peace that Lebanon had known or would know for a long time. Who but God could have foreseen that period of peace and arranged that the *Logos* be able to visit at just that time?

16

The rainbow in the sky

'The hunger for Bibles was evident from our first day in port,' wrote David Greenlee in the Port Report from Ushuaia, the southernmost city of Argentina. 'Pastors at the opening reception carried off tall stacks of the Scriptures, one of them taking over £120 worth! There is revival in Argentina and insufficient supply of God's word to meet the demand. Christian books and Bibles formed a high proportion of our total sales to over 9,000 visitors over the course of the visit.'

It was *Logos*' 401st port of call, and her arrival in Argentina brought to 103 the number of countries she had visited so far in her life as 'God's ship'. David Greenlee describes Ushuaia as 'one of the most spectacular ports ever visited by the *Logos*. Jagged mountain peaks tower over the narrow waterway, the mid-summer snowline only a few hundred metres above the sea. Though the sun dips below the horizon briefly late at night, the midnight glow on New Year's Eve seemed to draw the peaks even closer to our berth.'

On the evening of 4 January 1988, the *Logos* set sail southwards from Ushuaia. Her time of departure had originally been set at 4.00 p.m., but she had been delayed by a customs agent who insisted that certain papers were not in order. The affair was eventually cleared up, and just after 7.30 p.m. the ship finally set off on her journey through the notoriously treacherous waters of the Beagle Channel. Weather conditions were excellent. Visibility was good. Everything was in hand. The captain, however, was quite tired. He knew he would probably be up most of the night. The wise thing, he decided, would be to take advantage of the opportunity for a couple of hours of sleep before nightfall, which would occur quite late.

After giving careful instructions to the officer on duty and to the pilot that he should be called if weather conditions deteriorated or any other need arose, Captain Stewart went below to his cabin and immediately fell asleep. At 11.30 p.m. he was aroused from a deep sleep by the sound of the phone. Struggling back to consciousness, he reached for the receiver.

'Can you come up to the bridge immediately?' asked the voice of the second officer, the officer on duty.

Captain Stewart didn't have to look outside to know that weather conditions had deteriorated. The ship was listing to port. The wind, he sensed, was very strong. He could hear it howling overhead through the tops of the masts. Because the channel was narrow, there was not enough water surface exposed for the wind to act upon and cause huge waves. But that in no way meant that the wind was absent.

Still fighting to throw off the effects of a deep sleep and regain a fully alert mind, the captain made his way to the bridge. There he was greeted with the news that the pilot wanted to leave. A temporary pilot boat, large and awkward to manoeuvre, was trailing the *Logos*, waiting to pick up the pilot and transport him back to port. The skipper didn't want to risk his clumsy boat to the hazards of the heavy weather conditions that were blowing up. He had put pressure on the pilot to leave as quickly as possible while they were still in sheltered waters.

'But we're not through the channel yet,' objected the captain.

'The rest of the passage is quite safe,' the pilot assured him and quickly drew a track on the chart showing the route between the next two obstacles—the only remaining obstacles before the open sea, the tiny islands of Snipe and Solitario.

Captain Stewart knew that once the ship reached the open seas, she would get the full force of the winds which were building up to Force Eight or Nine. She would pitch and roll violently, but she was well prepared for sea. Everything— books, vehicles, all movable objects—was securely lashed down. It would be rough going for a few hours, but there would be no danger for the *Logos*.

The unwieldy pilot boat was in a different situation. Captain Stewart knew it would be difficult, if not impossible, to drop the pilot off in those conditions.

'Do I let him go or not?' The captain turned the question over in his mind. 'After all, there is just this one passage to get through. The pilot is the one who knows these waters. If he says it is safe . . .'

'All right,' agreed the captain somewhat reluctantly, 'if you are really sure it is safe for me to take this ship through, then I'm prepared to let you go.'

The pilot, visibly impatient to be on his way, assured him it was quite safe.

The pilot called his launch by VHF and then went down to a lower deck, accompanied by the second officer. The *Logos* set her main engine at dead slow while the launch tried to manoeuvre into position alongside the ship. The *Logos* was close to the shore and thus protected from the wind. The pilot launch was sheltered still further by going on the lee side of the *Logos*. In spite of this, the boat skipper seemed unable to bring his unwieldy craft alongside.

The pilot climbed down the customary pilot ladder, but each time he attempted to board the launch, waves lifted the boat up and swung it from the side of the ship. Hastily the pilot would scrambled back up the ladder to avoid getting his foot crushed. The pilot boat would then try to manoeuvre into position for another try. Finally, on the third attempt, the pilot let go of the ladder and jumped back into the boat, where someone quickly caught him. The pilot boat turned away from the *Logos* and headed back to Ushuaia.

The disembarkation of the pilot had taken eight or ten minutes. During that time the *Logos*, with her engines cut to dead slow to facilitate the manoeuvre, had drifted closer and closer to the southwest corner of Snipe Island. Relieved to finally get the pilot safely off, Captain Stewart immediately began to bear away from Snipe Island and to set the ship up to swing around clear of the island and head into the channel between Snipe and Solitario.

As the ship slowly swung around, Captain Stewart realised that the ship was getting alarmingly close to the visible part of Solitario. Immediately he gave orders to alter course to be sure to get around in time.

What happened next took Captain Stewart completely by surprise. The pilot, before he left, had given the captain clear instructions about the route to follow and had given some advice about using the radar equipment. The location of the islands, including the submerged parts, were clearly marked on the navigation chart. But there was another important hazard. A captain unfamiliar with these waters would know nothing about it. As the water was pressed from the northwest into the narrow channel between the two islands, it created a very strong current. The current pushed the ship with great force toward the rock shelf of Solitario Island. As the ship turned to pass between the islands, she also left the protection of the nearby shore and was suddenly hit broadside by the full force of the heavy winds from the southwest. Without making special allowance for these two powerful forces, the recommended course could not be held.

'That's strange,' exclaimed the captain in consternation, 'She's not making any progress!'

The ship seemed to stop. The feeling of standing still was so strong that the captain looked at the engine revolutions to

see if the engine had stopped. No, they were still at 105 rpm.
The captain realised then that they must be in the grip of a
very strong current indeed. In those one or two minutes the
ship had moved a couple of cables—more than a thousand
feet—to the right. With a series of heavy jarrings forward,
the ship struck the edge of the submerged rock shelf.

Hearing and feeling the collision, the captain immediately stopped the engines. The time was 11.55 p.m.

Always in the back of the mind of the Master of a vessel
there lurks the dread of a possible shipwreck. Suddenly,
without warning, the harrowing nightmare had become
reality. Feeling sick inside, Jonathan Stewart wished he
were somewhere else. But this was reality. The events *had*
happened and there was no way to undo them. He had to
face them and move on from there. Pushing from his mind
all thoughts of what might have been, Captain Stewart
concentrated his full attention on trying to free his vessel
from the present catastrophe.

Chief Engineer Dave Thomas was in his office resting and
waiting for the 'full away' signal after disembarking the
pilot. But instead of the expected signal came a sudden
grinding and intense vibration throughout the ship. Leaping
up, Dave rushed down to the engine room. On his way he
felt the main engine stop. He burst into the engine room.
Everything was in order. Benjamin, the engineer on duty,
had just pulled back the lever from the engine and was
calmly writing in the log book that the engine was astop.

Dave knew that something serious had happened. He had
felt those vibrations. His immediate thought was that the
ship must have hit something. Within minutes the rest of the
engine department had assembled in the engine room.
Automatically they began inspecting all the machinery
spaces for damage. There was none.

A phone call from the bridge sent Dave speeding up.
Captain Stewart met him in the wheelhouse with the words,
'It seems we've turned too late and caught some submerged
rocks. We seem to be aground.'

Dave was sent to check the rest of the ship for possible damage.

Down in hold number two Dave could see that the top of the water tank was bent up at one point. Shelves above it had collapsed by about nine inches, scattering books around. Clearly there was serious deformation under the ship, but no water was coming in.

Back in the engine room, the engineers took soundings of the water tank in number two hold. Brackish water came out of the sounding pipes. That meant that the tank had been pierced and sea water had entered the tank. The water tanks in hold number one could not be checked by sounding, but when the engineers tried to pump them out, the water level wouldn't go down. The water being pumped overboard was brackish. The engineers knew that these tanks too were open to the sea.

Dave went up to the bridge to report his findings and to discuss with the captain what should be done.

When a ship goes aground on sand or mud, she is cushioned to some extent against the violence of the elements. But a ship on rock gets the full force as the waves lift it and bring it crashing down with immense force against the hard, unyielding and often jagged surface of the rock. Many ships are pulled off a rock only to sink as soon as they are free. The *Logos* was pounding badly on the rock. Both the captain and Dave were fearful of subjecting her too long to such a brutal battering.

There were basically two courses of action open to him, the captain realised. He could leave the ship as it was and wait twenty-four hours for the next high tide, using the interval of time to summon a powerful tug to help pull the ship off. Or he could use the rising tide of two and a half metres, which would reach its peak in four or five hours, and try to get the ship free under her own power.

Dave suggested that the ship could be lightened by pumping out the number three tanks. With that and the rising tide, he and the captain were confident that they had a good chance of getting her off. Dave went below to supervise the long process of pumping out the water. Captain Stewart contacted the pilot and asked him to return to the *Logos* and use his detailed knowledge of the location to help in rescuing the ship.

About an hour after he had left the *Logos*, an obviously shaken pilot reboarded her.

'Why didn't you do as I said?' was his plaintive question.

'I did try to do as you said,' replied Captain Stewart curtly, 'but there is a very strong current through here, you know.'

There was no reply as the pilot paced up and down the bridge.

Ten minutes later a Chilean naval frigate captain came aboard to help, as the accident had occurred in Chilean waters. The Chilean captain was a highly qualified man, well-trained in salvage and ship damage. Furthermore, he knew the waters about as intimately as he knew his own home. The three men—the *Logos* captain, the pilot and the Chilean captain—formed a salvage team and fought desperately for the next four cr five hours to get the ship off. A naval tug from Ushuaia was requested to come to their assistance.

It was at this time that Judith Fredricsen, the girl in the ship's hospital, sat up and lifted her encased leg over the side of the bed so she could get up to investigate the noises that had woken her. She related what happened next:

'One of the guys came dashing down to the clinic to see if I was OK. At that stage he was telling all the people to get their life-jackets and go to the boatdeck. I was in the clinic, so I didn't know where my life-jacket was. He found it and then told one of the girls to keep an eye on me.

'In the boat drill you are always told to put on two pair of trousers, socks and everything. Well, I had this plaster on. There was no way I could get on a pair of trousers. The only thing I had in the clinic was a skirt, so I put that on. I guess that showed I didn't really think we were going to have to leave the ship.

'Then I hopped to my cabin, which was next door, and told the girls to throw me my blue jumper because it was my favourite one and I thought that if anything happened, I wanted to have that one. But she didn't speak English very well, so she threw me a different one. That turned out to be a good thing because it was a lot warmer.

'I hopped up to the dining-room and lounge area. Everyone was milling around. Nobody knew quite what to do. There was a real variety of reactions. Some people were obviously very scared. A young guy who had just joined was crying. A lot of people were totally blank. Others were smiling and carrying on like it couldn't be real. That's what I was doing. I wasn't really upset.

'The doctor came up and found me. She checked me over and gave me a bottle of pain killers in case I needed to walk on my foot.

'"Have you got any trousers?" she asked.

'"Well, I can't get anything on, can I, over the plaster?"

'"I'll go and get your jeans anyway. If we get in the lifeboats, we'll cut them or rip them and get them on you." '

David Greenlee and his wife Vreni had gone to bed about 11.00 p.m. When the crash came just before midnight, Vreni woke up asking, 'What is it? What is it?'

'I knew immediately that we'd crashed,' said David, and went on to describe what happened:

'We quickly pulled on our warm clothes and got our life-jackets on and got some warm clothes on Rebekka, our one-and-a-half-year-old daughter.

'An announcement was made to go to the dining-room, although apparently a number of people did not hear it. Now linked with that, I had a very clear sense that I had to lead the people in prayer and singing.

'The Anglican bishop in Punta Arenas had read from Psalm 61 in a service recently on board and I had just read it in my devotions. So we started off with that psalm. Tom Jarrett came up to the piano. This was all very spontaneous. I waited until I saw enough people there, perhaps fifty, but I had this sense we had to get started before people got talking or worried or whatever.

'I'd been talking to a guy that afternoon and the theme of peace with God came out. So there were a lot of verses fresh in my mind about peace. We began to pray for peace.'

Immanuel Böker was so keyed up he simply couldn't sit still throughout the prayer meeting. He got up and wandered down to see what was happening below in the holds.

'Hold number one was completely dry. In hold number two some books had fallen from the shelves, but not many. We started putting them back in order, but the carpenter said that wasn't necessary. We did it anyway.

'Every ten minutes we checked on the list of the ship. From one of the shelves someone had hung a pencil tied to a length of string to act as a plumb-line. Behind it was steel, coated with something silver. You could see pencil marks quite clearly on it. So we indicated the list there every ten minutes. I remember clearly how the ship tipped from side to side and then came upright again. It also rocked forward and backward, creaking as it moved. It would always stop with a bang as it slipped back and give another bang as it slid forward again.'

Most of the people not on duty eventually joined in the time of prayer and singing in the dining room and lounge area. The captain came down and gave a brief explanation of what had happened and what was being done. He assured the people there was nothing to worry about. In a few hours with high tide the ship should come free. Meanwhile the people could go back to their cabins if they wished. 'Just keep your life-jackets handy,' he warned.

Grantley Sherwood wrote:

'We fully expected that it was just a matter of time before we would be floating free again. We had hot chocolate and spent a wonderful time in prayer and praise.

'I then went back to bed to try and catch some sleep, as I had been asked to assist on the 4.00 a.m. to 8.00 a.m. watch duty. However I couldn't sleep, instinctively listening to the main engine labouring at full astern (reverse), occasionally broken by a scraping noise. This was accompanied by the engine racing as the ship would move back a few metres. It would be resumed by the engine again labouring as the propellor thrashed the water, desperately trying to free the ship from the rock's grasp. I felt like cheering the ship on, crying and pleading, getting out and pushing; anything to help her in her misery.'

Ursula Böker brought her two pre-school-aged children upstairs so she could participate in the prayer meeting. For half an hour or so they sat quietly in the laps of Ursula and another young woman. But when the dull stupor of suddenly-interrupted sleep wore off, they wriggled down from the laps and began to play and run around. The sharp angle of the floor provided great fun for sliding: They would go to the high side of the room and slide down to the lower side. For them, certainly, the situation held no terrors, no reason for fear or anxiety.

Most of the people on the ship could not believe that anything serious would happen to the ship. They had been reassured by the captain. This sense of confidence grew as the hours passed without any noticeable deterioration in the situation. David Greenlee was one of the few who were convinced from the first moment that the ship was lost. When asked later why he didn't bring his slides and camera, and so on, he answered:

'I was in my office at one point briefly to get a coat or something. I looked at my camera and I looked at my computer and I made a conscious decision. I looked at them and then I thought of my little daughter Rebekka and I said to myself, "There's no question."

'I left them behind because I didn't want to have anything that in any way would hinder me in carrying Rebekka. Even with my long arms I could barely hang on to her when wearing the thick, cumbersome life-jacket. We did put together a small bag with a few things later—my rechargeable shaver, toothbrushes, and so on. But things were just not important any more.'

During all of this time the engineers were trying to pump out the number three tanks. It took a very long time. Dave Thomas related the succeeding events from his point of view:

'We got the tank on the starboard empty. The port tank had just five tons or so in it. By about half-past four we felt quite light. We had the main engine running absolutely full astern with flames and everything pouring out of the stack. It felt as

though we were just ready to come off. During the time from
4.00 a.m. to 4.30 a.m. we could really feel the bumping in the
engine room spaces. It was under the port side and we knew that
something was happening down there. But it did feel as if the
ship was very, very nearly ready to lift off.

'Then about twenty-to-five I got a call from the bridge
requesting me to go straight down to number two hold. I went
down. There was some water coming in. It had started coming in
on the port side where the deformation had been. But it was not
leaking particularly much. As we stood there bouncing up and
down with the ship, water suddenly started to come in from a
point above us, the tween deck. I went up to see. Massive
quantities were coming in from the old obsolete sonar trunk
which had been blocked off underneath the ship.

'I rang the bridge and told the captain that the water was
coming in at such a rate that there was no way the pump was
going to be able to control it.'

The situation began deteriorating so rapidly that the
captain wanted everyone out of the cabins and up above,
dressed and ready to abandon ship if it became necessary.
Everyone was told to go up on deck on the starboard side.
Meanwhile the captain, his chief officer and the chief
engineer were conferring together on the bridge. They all
agreed that there was no longer a possibility of saving the
ship. She must be abandoned. The sooner everyone could
be got off, the better. At 5.00 a.m. the captain gave the order
to prepare the lifeboats. Ten minutes later he gave the order
to abandon ship.

During most of her time on the rock shelf, the ship had
been listing at an angle of about ten degrees. When the water
began pouring in, the list began to increase rapidly. By the
time the order to prepare lifeboats was given, the list had
reached seventeen degrees. By the end of an hour it would
be forty degrees.

This list was not just a matter of strange and unpleasant
conditions for the people on board as they tried to make
their way through the ship. It had serious implications for
their safety in disembarking from the ship. About thirty

people on board were certified to handle lifeboats. During their rigorous training period they had been told that all the things they were learning would apply and the lifeboats were designed to be lowered when the ship was listing up to as much as fifteen degrees. The *Logos* already lay at seventeen degrees and her list was rapidly increasing.

Every week the entire ship's company had been exercised in lifeboat drills and now that the emergency faced them, they knew exactly how they were supposed to be dressed, where they were supposed to go and what they were supposed to do. Quietly, methodically, their minds hardly able to accept that the situation was really happening, the people went through all the motions just as they had been trained. There was no panic, no screaming, no elbowing of anyone's way ahead of others.

The procedure for most of the boats was to lift the boat by means of winches off the blocks where it rested on deck, and swing it out over the water alongside the boat deck. People would climb into it as it was held in against the side of the ship. When everyone was inside, the boat would be lowered gently to the water. To give added security, three grablines were thrown over the side of the ship for people to hold on to. As many people as possible would keep their hands on these lifelines as the boat descended.

A rather straightforward operation in normal conditions. But the *Logos* wasn't in normal conditions. Because the ship was heeling over so far to the port side, the lifeboats did not hang as they should have done. The starboard boats were pressed hard against the ship's side while the port boats swung away, leaving a big gap of six or seven feet.

On the port side, the lower side of the ship, it was simply not possible for the people to get into the lifeboats. The two-and-a-half ton boats had to be heaved over to the side of the *Logos* and held securely in place before the occupants could board. Then the boats were slowly lowered to the water. For the people in them it was a terrifying experience to look up and see the ship looming over them, to realise they were not *alongside* the ship but *under* it, right in its path if it should keel over on top of them.

Andy Toncic went to his life station by way of the lower side of the ship. 'Upon reaching the boat deck,' he said, 'I realised the seriousness of our situation. The ship was listing so severely people were sliding down the deck almost into the lifeboats or off the ship.' When he reached his own lifeboat on the higher side of the ship, he found some men trying to throw overboard a container with a life-raft inside. He went to help. 'The listing,' he said, 'made it virtually impossible to lift. Four of us were trying desperately to throw it over into the water. The ship suddenly moved to the left, and the 300-pound container slipped from our hands. People were standing below the platform holding the container. Unbelievably no one was hit.'

As Andy's boat, lifeboat number one, was lowered, it caught on the edge of the lifeboat deck and suddenly tilted. Everyone was holding on to a grabline and nobody fell out.

'What can we do now?' asked the shocked occupants.

'Why don't we get everyone to climb out on the deck?' suggested someone. 'Then while the boat is being lowered we can try to push it out far enough to get past the obstacle.' Acting on this suggestion, the boat coxswain directed the lifeboat men to help the people back onto the deck. Then three men perched on the rail of the ship and placed their feet against the lifeboat. As the boat was lowered, they pushed with all their strength. The boat glided safely past the obstacle. Hardly had it done so than with a sudden, forceful lurch it swung into the open alleyway of the deck below. Had people been in the boat, they could have been flung out into the icy waters below. As it was, some of the men were able to push the boat out and ease it past the railing. There it stopped to allow the people to climb back in.

The problems were not over, however. Directly in the path of the descending boat the water from the cooling system was discharging from the side of the ship. Water was gushing out. No one relished the idea of getting soaked, and possibly having the boat flooded, but there was no way to avoid it. As the boat neared the discharge, the flow of water suddenly stopped. Without mishap, the boat continued on its way and reached the sea safely. The lowering gear was released and the boat moved away toward ships waiting to pick up the survivors. In the lifeboat were the two pre-school-aged children of the Böker family. They found the situation inordinately interesting. Solome, usually so fearful in strange situations, was laughing and stamping her feet against the bottom of the boat.

Judith Fredricsen was in boat number three on the high side:

'I gave up hopping at that stage. There was no way I could climb into a lifeboat and protect my foot. So I just jumped in. After the mothers and children, everybody made way for me. I didn't really think I was so crippled that I needed to go ahead of anyone, but people were very calm and very considerate.

'Lifeboat number one, which was forward of us, had difficulties. When they tried to lower the boat, they swung in and got stuck. Our men told us, "There's no point in us doing the same. Get out and go down to the next deck and we'll load you in from that deck."

'That's when I first started to worry. I thought, what if we don't have time to get down there and reload?

'To get to the steps we had to cross the wet, slippery deck of the outside cafeteria area. All the benches had slid down to the lower side of the deck. There was nothing to hold on to. Most people would wait until the ship was sort of steady and make a run for it. I couldn't run. A couple of people did actually fall and slip right down to the side of the ship. I was pretty scared that I was going to slip, but I held on to somebody and we made it.

'We went down the stairs and around the passageway and then I thought, "Oh no!" Because the lifeboat was on a level with the rail. You didn't just step in. You had to get up and then down into the boat. Someone helped me. I just basically got thrown into the boat.'

Lifeboat number three was the last boat to pull away from the ship because it carried the captain. The chief engineer, too was in that boat. As he watched lifeboat number one being lowered, Dave Thomas exclaimed in dismay, 'Oh dear, I need to shut off the generators to stop the cooling water discharge!'

'Is it possible to do that?' asked the captain.

'Yes, but I've got to go down to the settling tanks flat to do it and shut it off at the tanks.'

He rushed down and was back in a couple of minutes.

'That's it,' he announced. 'Everything's shut off. Praise the Lord!'

It was this action which had saved lifeboat number one from being flooded by the water discharge pouring out the side of the ship.

All six of the lifeboats reached the water safely. The two that were fitted with engines motored around and collected the others that had cleared the ship using their oars. The unused life-rafts were collected as well. In tow they all set out for the Chilean naval boats about a quarter of a mile away. By 5.30 a.m., thirty minutes after the call to prepare lifeboats, everyone was safely aboard the waiting vessels.

'The reaction I've had from many letters I have received,' said the captain later, 'has been incredulity that we got off without a scratch. "How did you do it? You must be extremely well-trained to achieve such a thing because it rarely happens that way. Even experienced seamen get hurt." Well, I believe God took care of us.'

As the lifeboats were heading toward the naval vessels, *Logos* people looked back to watch the *Logos* recede into the distance. Only then did the full impact hit many of them. They would never again see the ship that had been home to them for months or even years. Grantley Sherwood expressed his feelings this way:

'Once aboard the Navy vessel I looked back at the *Logos;* then I knew that her sailing days were over. I just started to weep as the full realisation of everything hit me. Siyabullela (from Cape Town) buried his head into my shoulder and started to pray for me. I joined in prayer and within minutes I felt God's joy and peace flood me through and through. Spontaneously all of us started to sing "God is so good . . . he's so good to me." Right there in the belly of the Navy vessel we had a really dynamic time of praise and worship. God had been so faithful: he kept the ship safe right throughout the dark of the night and the high wind. Only when it was safe to abandon ship did he allow the water in. He made sure that every life was saved against impossible odds and even made sure that we could have breakfast in Puerto Williams. We hadn't even missed a single meal—isn't he just fantastic?'

When David Greenlee had gone out on the poop deck of the *Logos* early that morning he had seen a most brilliant rainbow in the sky. 'Amazingly brilliant,' he commented. 'I had read Ezekiel 1:28 just two or three weeks ago. Ezekiel had been in the Lord's presence and had said, "Like the appearance of a rainbow in the clouds on a rainy day, so was the radiance around him. This was the appearance of the likeness of the glory of the Lord." '

The rainbow was still in the sky as the people pulled away from the *Logos*. Its arc spread across the sky and curved downward to come to an end right where the *Logos* lay mortally wounded and deserted.

Epilogue—the end of the beginning

A hundred and thirty-nine people were evacuated from the *Logos*, people ranging in age from fifty-nine years to six weeks. In spite of the adverse conditions not a single person was injured. Taken by the Chilean Navy to the nearest Chilean port, the tiny naval outpost of Puerto Williams, they were received with warm blankets, food, accommodation and much warmth and friendliness.

Within three days most of the *Logos* company was flown out to Punta Arenas, a small city in the south-ernmost part of Chile. Churches of different denominations in Punta Arenas responded to the crisis in a beautiful demonstration of compassion, love and unity. Opening up their homes to the stranded ship personnel, they found places for everyone to live and enjoy the warm support of caring people.

A few days later they were transported to Buenos Aires in Argentina, where a Bible college provided facilities for everyone to be together as a ship group but apart from other people. For the ship's company this was a very important time. For days they had been moving around in a state of shock. They needed an opportunity to come to terms with what had happened. Several OM leaders flew to Buenos Aires to be with them during this time of personal crisis to offer counsel and support.

Even though the *Logos* had been several hours on the rock shelf, the call to abandon ship came so unexpectedly and with such urgency that the men and women had no chance to collect things from their cabins. Most of them left the ship with just the clothes on their bodies. A few had cameras because they had been taking photos during the time of crisis. But they had very little else. Not only did they leave behind clothes, musical instruments, tape recorders and so forth, but many things that could never be replaced, such as diaries, address books, Bible study notes, photos, and souvenirs with very personal memories.

Grantley Sherwood wrote, 'In Puerto Williams I learned a new aspect of sharing: fifty guys to four towels, ten to a comb, two or three to a toothbrush. My toothbrush buddy was Mike from the USA.'

In Punta Arenas and in Buenos Aires they were given a small amount of money to be able to purchase some of the basic necessities. Christians not only in these places but in Puerto Montt, Chile and farther away in Panama and the United States immediately responded by sending clothes, many of them brand new. From many sources came money designated for replacing lost articles.

Even more difficult than the loss of material possessions for many was the loss of a home. Some of the workers had been on the *Logos* only a few weeks. For others it had been home for a year, two years or even longer. Chief Engineer Dave Thomas had sailed on the *Logos* on her maiden voyage seventeen years earlier. While on the *Logos* he had met his wife, married, and begun rearing a family. For the better part of seventeen years he had poured himself into maintaining, repairing and improving the ship. In every sense of the word it was home for him.

While the others were boarding the naval vessels to be transported to Puerto Williams, Dave and Chief Officer

Tom Dyer returned to the *Logos*. Three others went with them but did not remain. There was a legal reason for their presence aboard the ship or in the vicinity on a naval vessel. 'But that was not the real reason,' Dave said. 'I stayed because I didn't want to leave her. Even if I could not do anything to rescue her, I just wanted to be there anyway.'

It was two weeks before the two men rejoined their families in Punta Arenas. During this time the men on the Chilean naval vessel standing by were very sympathetic, doing everything they could to help Dave and Tom through this difficult time. Whenever it was decided that the situation on *Logos* was too dangerous, Dave and Tom were invited on board the naval ship until conditions improved.

Probably the man who suffered most was Captain Jonathan Stewart. The *Logos* had had a very public ministry and he could not help but wonder about the consequences worldwide. So many Christians had been involved in the ministry and would feel the loss of the ship keenly.

Arriving in Puerto Williams, he was given a formal invitation to the officers' wardroom and had his meals there. Later he said, 'It was so good for me personally to be sheltered in the bond of officers who said, "Look, we've done these things too." They treated me as a fellow officer. They didn't have to do that. It really helped me more than I can say.'

For several days Captain Stewart and everyone who had been on the bridge at the time of the accident were involved in a hard, intensive investigation by the Chilean naval authorities. The Port Captain, under pressure because of the international significance of the event, was very strict, very professional.

'It absolutely exhausted me,' said Captain Stewart. 'If people had not been praying so fervently for me, I think I would have just gone to pieces with the emotion and the pressure of it all.'

The report of that very thorough investigation was sent to the naval authorities in Santiago, the capital. Their decision after studying the report was that no charges should be brought against the captain, the ship owners or the pilot involved.

Because the ship was in such an isolated place, the cost of trying to salvage the things aboard would have been exorbitant. Just disposing of the ship itself so as not to endanger the shipping lane could have been tremendously expensive. Mike Poynor, now the man in charge of all technical matters for the OM ships, decided that the best solution was to see if the Chilean Navy would be willing to take the ship as it was, assuming all responsibility for it in exchange for the right of salvage. Other OM leaders agreed. The Chilean Navy accepted the offer. On 26 January the *Logos* was officially delivered to the Chilean Navy.

No one in OM was prepared for the response of people around the world to the news of the disaster. One phone at the naval outpost was constantly in use as Graham Wells, the ship director, devoted himself to answering calls of reporters. For days the accident was featured in the news in Britain. OM leaders tried to get a message through to the sister ship, the *Doulos*, but were unable to do so because she was at sea at the time; her radio officer was shocked to pick up the shattering news from a BBC newscast. From all over the world calls came into the ship headquarters checking to see if the unbelievable news was really true.

While OMers involved with the ship were still numb from shock and trying to deal with the immediate problems of the people who had been evacuated and the ship itself, Christians in many parts of the world were looking ahead into the future. The feeling of many of these believers was expressed by someone who wrote, 'The *Logos* was not just an OM ship, it was *our* ship!'

Countless lives had been significantly altered through the ministry of the *Logos*. That ministry could not be allowed to die away with the loss of the *Logos*. Surely God must have taken away the *Logos* to provide a larger ship more adequate for the work! Taking the initiative in their own hands, Christians began giving and challenging others to give to replace the *Logos*.

When a church in Brazil took an offering, many people were so moved they took off their watches and jewellery and laid them in the offering plate. One of the first gifts in the United States came from children who had saved their nickels and dimes. In Britain, as well as in other countries, Christian leaders from different churches, Christian organisations and missions united in an appeal for funds, saying as someone put it, 'Many missionary societies have benefited from people who gained a vital part of their training on board one of the OM ships' (*Evangelism Today*, March, 1988).

Many people wrote to the ship headquarters expressing their sympathy and encouragement. This word came from Mr Bayo Famonure, Chief Executive of Calvary Ministries in Nigeria:

> 'We send our heart-felt sympathy over the loss of *Logos* . . . . The Lord allows certain things to happen to us which we may not fully understand, but we know that our Redeemer lives, and will glorify himself in all situations . . .
>
> 'There is a Nigerian proverb that says: when the palace of a chief or a king catches fire, it paves the way for a better and a modern one. We sincerely pray that this will apply to *Logos*; that the loss of *Logos* will pave the way for another and better ship.'

Note

On 23 September 1988, Operation Mobilisation announced the signing of a £1.15 million (sterling) purchase agreement for the 4900-ton Greek-owned car/passenger ferry *Argo*, which was to be renamed *Logos II*. The loss of *Logos* did indeed pave the way for another and better ship.

Postscript: God did provide another ship, larger and much better suited for the ministry. Ten months after the Logos accident, a 20-year-old Spanish ferry was purchased, christened Logos II and taken to Amsterdam, Holland for extensive renovation. Several hundred volunteers from many parts of the world braved the biting cold, the incessant assault of ear-blasting noises and the ubiquitous grime and dust to contribute their part to the transformation. Finally, on the 24th of April 1990 the Logos II, gleaming white against a bright blue sky, set sail for her first port of call: Tilbury Docks, London, England.

God's timing, as always, was perfect. Just as the Logos II was being launched into ministry, Communism was losing its grip on the countries of Eastern Europe. Logos II was able to visit East Germany, Poland, Russia, Latvia and Lithuania as one of the first highly public emissaries of God's church.

Logos was gone but its ministry was not. God was giving a glimpse of the great plans He had in store for a ship called Logos II.

Facts and figures

Between October 1970 (Copenhagen, Denmark) and January 1988 (Ushuaia, Argentina) *Logos* sailed 231,250 nautical miles and made a total of 401 port visits in 258 different ports, in 103 countries.

During that time an estimated 7.48 million people visited the book exhibition and 370,000 attended meetings on board. In addition, more than 2 million people attended meetings on shore where ship personnel ministered. Over 4,000 men and women participated in the training programme on board.

Of the estimated 51 million pieces of Christian literature distributed 450,000 were Bibles or New Testaments. Approximately 1.6 million Christian books and 3.5 million educational books were sold.

Thousands indicated a decision to commit their lives to Jesus Christ as Lord and Saviour. Many others have testified that their call into Christian work came through the *Logos* ministry.

Built	1949 Denmark
Tonnage	2319
Dimensions	
Length	82 m
Breadth	13.44 m
Draught	5.5 m
Capacity – Persons	144

Captains

Bjørn Kristiansen	Norway	October 1970–October 1972
George Paget	UK	October 1972–May 1977
Jonathan Stewart	UK	May 1977–October 1977
George Paget	UK	October 1977–June 1978
Neil Porter	UK	June 1978–March 1979
Simon Cheeren	India	March 1979–May 1979
Pertti Merisalo	Finland	May 1979–June 1980
Dennys Collins	UK	June 1980–February 1981
Tage Benson	Sweden	February 1981–July 1981
Pertti Merisalo	Finland	August 1981–August 1983
Dietrich Krieghoff	Germany	August 1983–September 1983
Pertti Merisalo	Finland	September 1983–March 1984
Tage Benson	Sweden	March 1984–May 1985
Dallas Parker	USA	May 1985–June 1985
Jonathan Stewart	UK	June 1985–May 1986
Dallas Parker	USA	May 1986–September 1986

Jonathan Stewart	UK	September 1986–July 1987
Tom Dyer	USA	August 1987–October 1987
Jonathan Stewart	UK	October 1987–January 1988

Chief Engineers

John Yarr	Australia	October 1970–February 1973
Mike Poynor	USA	February 1973–April 1975
Rex Worth	UK	April 1975–December 1975
Mike Poynor	USA	December 1975–July 1976
Dave Thomas	UK	August 1976–November 1978
Leen Schotte	Holland	December 1978–August 1980
Johannes Thomsen	Denmark	September 1980–October 1982
Dave Thomas	UK	October 1982–December 1985
Elon Alva	India	December 1985–January 1986
Dave Thomas	UK	January 1986–November 1986
Elon Alva	India	December 1986–March 1987
Dave Thomas	UK	March 1987–January 1988

Directors

George Verwer	USA	October 1970–October 1971
George Miley	USA	October 1971–January 1976 (during this period George Verwer relieved George Miley on several occasions)
Dave Hicks	USA	January 1976–May 1976
George Miley	USA	June 1976–May 1977
Dave Hicks	USA	June 1977–March 1980
Allan Adams	Australia	April 1980–October 1984
Frank Fortunato	USA	October 1984–October 1985
Manfred Schaller	Germany	November 1985–October 1987
Graham Wells	UK	October 1987–January 1988

International Address: OM Ships, Postfach 1609, D-6950 Mosbach, West Germany.

U.S. Address: OM LIT, P.O. Box 28 Waynesboro, GA 30830